# ROSE GUIDE TO
# GENESIS

R SE
PUBLISHING

Rose Guide to Genesis
©2023 Rose Publishing

Published by Rose Publishing
An imprint of Tyndale House Ministries
Carol Stream, Illinois
www.hendricksonrose.com

ISBN 978-1-4964-7799-6

Contributing authors: Paul H. Wright, PhD (chapter 2: *The Book of Genesis;* chapter 5: *Noah's Ark*) and Danielle Parish, MDiv (chapter 4: *Understanding the World of Genesis*); chapter 3: *Genesis Time Line* (Rose Publishing, 2012); chapter 6: *Abraham: A Journey of Faith* (Rose Publishing, 2015); chapter 7: *Life of Joseph: God's Purposes in Suffering* (Rose Publishing, 2010)

Some photos and illustrations used under license from Shutterstock.com and from *Family Time in Bible Pictures* by Tyndale House Publishers, Inc.

Printed in the United States of America
010423VP

# CONTENTS

# CHAPTER 1

# The Story of Genesis

**A**ll stories have a beginning. The story of the Bible starts not with the "once upon a time" of fairy tales, but with four other unforgettable words: "In the beginning God ..." (Gen. 1:1). This story begins with God. Before the existence of the world as we know it today, before thousands of years of human history, before even the formation of galaxies and planets, there was God. Genesis, the first book of the Bible, is the account of how all good things in this world began, and how so much of it went terribly wrong.

## THE STORY OF GENESIS AT A GLANCE

### Creation (Gen. 1–2)

> Now the earth was formless and empty, darkness was over the surface of the deep, and the Spirit of God was hovering over the waters. And God said, "Let there be light, and there was light."
>
> GENESIS 1:2–3

The first chapter of Genesis tells how God brought form to the formless and filled the emptiness with life. With the power of his word, God created light where there was none, put galaxies in space, made birds to fill the air and fish to fill the seas, and like a potter at his wheel, he formed the first human being from the dust of the ground.

The creation story reveals who God is. He is the Creator who gives life to humanity and all living things. This world is his beautiful and "very good" creation (Gen. 1:31). In the first two chapters of Genesis, we see God as designer, artist, architect, and life-giver—a good and loving God who takes delight in his creation. He needs nothing, yet freely gives life to all.

The creation story also tells us something about ourselves. We are not here by accident. Our Creator purposefully designed us to reflect himself.

God created mankind in his own image, in the image of God he created them; male and female he created them.

GENESIS 1:27

He made the first man Adam from the dust of the ground, and the first woman Eve from Adam's side. As image-bearers of God, their directive was an important one: to fill the earth and reign over God's creation.

## A Fallen World (Gen. 3–5)

The first two chapters of Genesis portray a picture of the world that is "very good" (Gen. 1:31). God put the first man and woman in the garden of Eden, a place where they cared for God's creation and God cared for them. Both Adam and Eve were naked and felt no shame (Gen. 2:25).

Consider the world as it is today. It is easy to see that many things are not the way they should be. If everything was once so good, how did it go so wrong? The next chapter in Genesis answers this question.

Adam and Eve had a choice: trust in the goodness of their Creator or go their own way, rebelling against the kind of life God had given them. God issued them one restriction: "You must not eat from the tree of the knowledge of good and evil, for when you eat from it you will certainly die" (Gen. 2:17).

Deceived by a manipulative serpent, Eve chose the fruit of the one tree that was off limits. (Revelation 12:9 and 20:2 point to the involvement of Satan—"that ancient serpent"—in this deception in the garden.) Adam also ate the fruit, and things were never the same. Shame, followed by hiding

from God, was their immediate response (Gen. 3:7–8). The man and woman had known only the goodness of God. In rebellion against their Maker, they came to know evil as well.

They tried to hide from God, but it was no use. Sinful choices have consequences. The first couple—and all humanity thereafter—was banished from the garden of Eden. Sinfulness, corruption, pain, and death entered the world. Life became very difficult: physical pain, hard work, broken relationships with each other and with God, and ultimately death. The world was no longer the way it should be. The following stories in the book of Genesis give a clear—and at times disturbing—portrait of the effects of sin.

## Noah's Ark (Gen. 6–11)

By chapter six in Genesis, many years had passed since Adam and Eve, and the human race increased rapidly, but so did evil, corruption, and violence (Gen. 6:5, 12). The Creator who had given life in the first chapters of Genesis concludes that the wickedness of humanity is so great that he will take away all the life he had made on the face of the earth. The means of destruction will be a massive flood like the world had never seen before!

The flood story can be viewed as a kind of reverse creation story. It is the undoing of the created world that had become so corrupted.

Yet there was one man who had found favor with God. Noah, whose name may mean "comfort" or "relief," was a righteous and blameless person who walked with God (Gen. 6:8–9). God chose to save Noah and his family from God's wrath against evil in the world. In a way, the life-destroying flood would bring about a new start for humanity, another beginning.

By faith, Noah did exactly as God instructed and built a large ark. Then the flood waters came and covered the entire earth. For one year, Noah, his family, and many pairs of animals survived inside the ark. All other life on the land was destroyed. The breath of life we read about earlier in Genesis is snuffed out, save for a few on the ark. Finally, the waters receded and Noah and his family and all the animals exited the ark.

God made an everlasting covenant with Noah and all living creatures. He declared that never again would he destroy the earth in a flood. The rainbow in the sky would be the "sign of the covenant," a reminder that God will keep his promise (Gen. 9:12–17). Though it was a new beginning, the fallen state of humanity and of the world continued. It was not long before Noah and his family were acting sinfully and reaping the consequences.

## Abraham and Sarah (Gen. 12–24)

Even with a new beginning after the flood waters were gone, sin and corruption remained in the world. Much of humanity continued living against the will of God. Yet God was undeterred from bringing about his plan to redeem humanity and all creation. Starting in Genesis 12, we see God forging a path of redemption through one special—though far from perfect—family. The story of this family begins with a childless couple named Abraham and Sarah.

Abraham and his wife Sarah (also called Abram and Sarai) were originally from the ancient city of Ur in Mesopotamia. Ur, as we know from archaeology, was a thriving center of commerce. But it was also a city teeming with the worship of false gods. Abraham's family was semi-nomadic, moving to wherever they could find food and pasturelands for their flocks. They traveled from Ur to Harran in upper Mesopotamia, another major city of commerce.

God called Abraham to migrate from Harran to the land of Canaan. God assured Abraham with a covenant that God would bless him and his family.

> The LORD had said to Abram, "Go from your country, your people and your father's household to the land I will show you. I will make you into a great nation, and I will bless you; I will make your name great, and you will be a blessing."
>
> GENESIS 12:1–2

Throughout Abraham's story in Genesis, God reaffirms this covenant on seven different occasions. The covenant included these promises: Abraham and Sarah would have a son (Gen. 18:1–15); all nations would be blessed through Abraham's descendants (Gen. 12:1–3); the land that God would show Abraham would belong to his descendants (Gen. 12:7; 22:15–18); and Abraham's descendants would be as numerous as the stars in the sky and the sand on the seashore (Gen. 13:14–17;15:1–21; 17:1–21; 22:17).

By faith, Abraham and his family left a thriving pagan city and followed God to a new and strange land. Genesis tells us that Abraham's faith in God's promise was "credited to him as righteousness" (Gen. 15:6). The book of Hebrews in the New Testament explains it this way:

> By faith Abraham, when called to go to a place he would later receive as his inheritance, obeyed and went, even though he did not know where he was going. By faith he made his home in the promised land like a stranger in a foreign country…. For he was looking forward to the city with foundations, whose architect and builder is God.
>
> HEBREWS 11:8–10

But there was a problem—at least from a human point of view. Abraham and Sarah were old and childless. How could they have a multitude of descendants, let alone even one descendant? God was promising them the impossible. In the ancient world, infertility was considered cause for a husband to divorce his wife or to have heirs through concubines or slaves. Rather than continue to wait for God's promise to be fulfilled,

Abraham, at Sarah's urging, had a son through Sarah's slave Hagar. Despite their attempt to shortcut God's promises, God kept his covenant, and Sarah, well-advanced in age, bore a son named Isaac. God was faithful to the covenant, but it was according to his timetable, not theirs. In fact, Isaac was born a full twenty-five years after God had first made the covenant with Abraham (Gen. 12:4; 21:5).

Abraham's faith in God must have increased after Isaac's birth, because when God told Abraham to do the unthinkable—to sacrifice his only son Isaac—Abraham was willing. Before Abraham could go through with it, God stopped him and provided a ram as the sacrifice instead. In this divine test, Abraham demonstrated great faith, believing that "God could even raise the dead" (Heb. 11:19).

## Jacob's Family (Gen. 25–36)

After Abraham's and Sarah's deaths, the Genesis narrative turns to Isaac's twin sons Jacob and Esau—but particularly Jacob. At birth, Jacob was given his name, translated as "he grasps at the heel," an ancient Hebrew expression that means "he deceives" (Gen. 25:26). Later in Jacob's life, God changed his name to Israel which means "struggles with God" (Gen. 32:28). Both names suggest a man (and also a family) in a tug-of-war with God and each other.

The stories in this section of Genesis detail how God's chosen family struggled. They struggled with God—Jacob did so, literally in Genesis 32. They struggled with each other—deceiving, fearing, and betraying. Some were victims, others were victimizers, and some were both. Most times they focused on their own survival, status, and power. For example, Jacob and his mother Rebekah tricked an aged and blind Isaac into giving Jacob the blessing that by custom belonged to Esau (Gen. 27:1–45). Jacob fled when Esau vowed revenge. It would be twenty years before the brothers would meet again. Jacob was fooled by Laban, who tricked him into marrying Leah when Jacob had wanted to marry Rachel. The deceiver had become the deceived. In the end, Jacob married both sisters (Gen. 29:15–30). (Having multiple wives was a common practice in the ancient world.) Leah and Rachel competed for their husband's affection by having as many children for him as possible—twelve sons and one daughter in total. They even gave their slave women to their husband to have children through them, much like Sarah had done with Hagar two generations earlier (Gen. 29:31–30:24).

There were, however, times when this family turned toward God, and God turned toward them. Jacob received an amazing glimpse into the heavenly realm, a dream of a stairway to heaven. The Lord reassured Jacob that the promises made to his grandfather Abraham would be fulfilled. An awestruck Jacob declared, "How awesome is this place!... The Lord will be my God" (Gen. 28:10–22). After twenty years of estrangement from his brother Esau, Jacob returned to Canaan and encountered Esau. Fearing for his life, Jacob humbled himself and prayed to God for protection. Much to Jacob's surprise, Esau did not take revenge, but instead embraced and forgave Jacob (Gen. 32:1–33:4). The Lord renewed his covenantal promises of blessing with this family despite their repeated failings (Gen. 26:3–5; 28:13–15). God chose to work his will through their broken lives, rescuing them from certain doom when their lies and foolishness got them in trouble.

## Joseph in Egypt (Gen. 37–50)

Against the backdrop of this very flawed family, the story of Joseph stands out. The book of Genesis devotes about thirteen chapters (that is approximately one fourth of the book) to the story of Joseph. His story provides us with an example of a young man from an unstable family who chose to rely on God when so much of his future seemed hopeless.

Joseph's older brothers resented him. As the biological son of Rachel, the wife Jacob loved most, Joseph was favored by his father. Also, God gave Joseph special dreams, which Joseph unwisely relayed to his brothers. His siblings understood Joseph's dreams to mean that one day they would all bow down to him—their little brother! Joseph's brothers were determined to make sure that would never happen. They sold him to slave traders and told their father that Joseph had been killed by a wild animal.

As a slave in Egypt, Joseph had no connections, no money, no status, and no protection from harm. But he did have someone on his side: "The LORD was with Joseph" (Gen. 39:2, 3, 21, 23). That made all the difference. Joseph did not just survive in this foreign land, he thrived. He was put in charge of the whole household of Potiphar, one of Pharaoh's officers.

As we can see from the rest of the Bible, God's plan was even bigger than what Abraham and Sarah may have understood. Not only would their descendants be numerous, but the Messiah, Jesus the Savior, would be born through Abraham's lineage. Genesis tells not only about the beginning of the nation of Israel through a son promised to Abraham and Sarah, but it also explains the beginning of a history which would ultimately lead to Christ Jesus, the Son of God.

But then Joseph suffered another injustice. He was thrown into prison after Potiphar's wife falsely accused him. He had done no wrong but once again found himself in chains. Yet the Lord was still with him. God gave Joseph the ability to interpret dreams—a blessing for which he gave God all the credit (Gen. 41:16). He interpreted Pharaoh's dreams about seven years of good harvest followed by seven years of famine. Pharaoh was so impressed that he released Joseph from prison and put him in charge of storing food for the people to survive the coming famine. Joseph became a top official in Egypt. The Lord was indeed with Joseph.

When his brothers traveled to Egypt to buy food during the famine, Joseph was faced with a choice: forgiveness or revenge. Unlike some others in his family tree had done before, Joseph chose forgiveness. He tested his brothers' sincerity and character with some deceit of his own, hiding his true identity. But in the end, he stopped the deception, revealed who he really was, and forgave his brothers entirely. Joseph understood that God had a bigger plan that would succeed in spite of human sinfulness. Looking back on all that had happened in his life, he declared to his brothers:

> You intended to harm me, but God intended it for good
> to accomplish what is now being done, the saving of
> many lives.
>
> GENESIS 50:20

The book of Genesis ends with God's chosen family living in Egypt. Jacob and his family had migrated to Egypt to escape the famine. Though they grew in number, as God's covenant said they would, they were far from the land God had promised. We read in the last chapter of Genesis that, though Joseph had made a new home for himself in Egypt, he wanted to be buried in the promised land (Gen. 50:25). This demonstrated Joseph's trust that God would be faithful to fulfill the promises he made so many years earlier to Abraham.

## GOD'S PLAN FOR REDEMPTION

In the book of Genesis, we see God acting sovereignly within his creation to bring about his plan of redemption:

☩ God is the creator of all things, the world, the nations, and Israel. Creation begins a story of relationships. God wants to relate to his creation, especially to humans.

☩ Although God created all things good and was pleased with them, humans abused their freedom and, because of sin, broke their relationship with God, with each other, and with nature.

☩ However, God's grace extended to humanity. Instead of leaving them in their rebellion and corruption, God promised to act directly to solve the human predicament. Genesis 3:15 foreshadows the coming of the one who would crush the head of the deceiving serpent: "I will put enmity between you and the woman, and between your offspring and hers; he will crush your head, and you will strike his heel." On the cross, Christ Jesus crushed Satan's head.

☩ God began his plan of restoration by choosing the family of Abraham to start over. God made a covenant with Abraham. God relates, guides, rescues, and provides for the family he has chosen.

# DAYS OF CREATION GENESIS 1:1–2:3

**DAYS OF FORMING**

**Day 1:** God creates day and night by dividing light from the darkness.

**Day 2:** God creates the sky and waters by separating the waters.

**Day 3:** God creates the seas and dry land by gathering the waters together. God makes vegetation to grow on the land.

**DAYS OF FILLING**

**Day 4:** God creates the sun, moon, and stars to fill the day and the night.

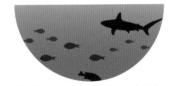

**Day 5:** God creates birds to fill the skies and fish to fill the seas.

**Day 6:** God creates animals and humans to fill the land.

**Day 7:** God rests on the seventh day and blesses it and makes it holy.

# LIFE SPANS FROM ADAM TO ABRAHAM
GENESIS 5:1–32; 11:10–26; 25:7

**ADAM** lived for 930 years.

**SETH** lived for 912 years.

**ENOSH** lived for 905 years.

**KENAN** lived for 910 years.

**MAHALALEL** lived for 895 years.

**JARED** lived for 962 years.

**ENOCH** lived for 365 years, then God took him.

**METHUSELAH** lived for 969 years.

**LAMECH** lived for 777 years.

**NOAH** lived for 950 years.

• **THE FLOOD** (Noah at age 600)

**SHEM** lived for 600 years.

**ARPHAXAD** lived for 438 years.

**SHELAH** lived for 433 years.

**EBER** lived for 464 years.

**PELEG** lived for 239 years.

**REU** lived for 239 years.

**SERUG** lived for 230 years.

**NAHOR** lived for 148 years.

**TERAH** lived for 205 years.

**ABRAHAM** lived for 175 years.

The lines in this chart indicate the length of the person's life in relation to the others.

# GENESIS TIME LINE

◆ Promise    ✷ Event    ▲ Move    ■ Birth    ● Death      Dates are approximate.

**Chapter 1**    ✷ God creates the world and everything in it.

**Chapter 2**    ✷ After creating Adam, the first man, God places him in the garden of Eden between the Tigris and Euphrates Rivers. Adam names all the animals.

✷ God forms Eve, Adam's wife, from one of Adam's ribs.

**Chapter 3**    ✷ Adam and Eve are cast out of Eden for sinning against God.

**Chapter 4**    ■ Cain and Abel are born to Adam and Eve.

✷ Cain murders Abel out of jealousy and is cast away by God to the land of Nod.

**Chapter 5**    ■ Shem, Ham, and Japheth are born to Noah.

**Chapter 6**    ✷ Construction of the ark begins.

**Chapter 7**    ✷ The Flood; Noah and his family are saved in the ark.

**Chapters 8-9**    ◆ God promises to never destroy the world again by a flood. Sign of the covenant is a rainbow.

**Chapter 10**    ▲ Descendants of Noah increase and form nations.

**Chapter 11**    ✷ Tower of Babel is built. God confuses the languages of the people so they cannot communicate with each other. As a result, the people scatter to different lands.

**Chapter 12**    ▲ Abram's father Terah plans to move his family from Ur to Canaan. Settles in Harran (midway).

◆ **God's First Promise to Abram**
God promises to make Abram into a great nation and that he will bless him and make his name great.

▲ God tells Abram to leave, so Abram leaves Harran for Canaan taking with him his wife Sarai, his nephew Lot, and all of his possessions and servants (2091 BC).

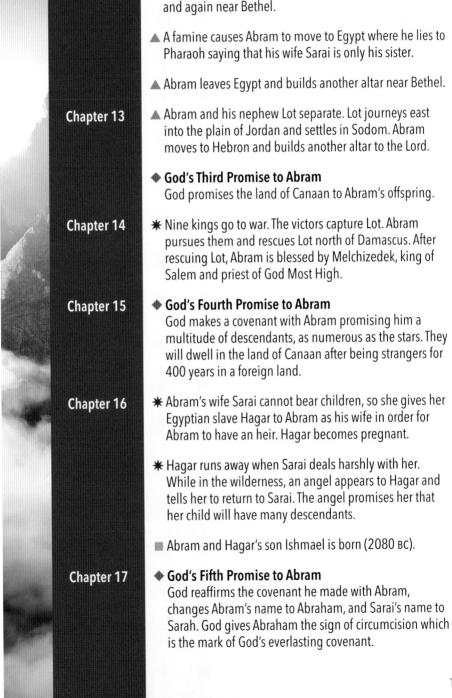

### ◆ God's Second Promise to Abram
Once in Canaan, God promises the land to Abram's offspring. Abram builds an altar to the Lord in Shechem and again near Bethel.

▲ A famine causes Abram to move to Egypt where he lies to Pharaoh saying that his wife Sarai is only his sister.

▲ Abram leaves Egypt and builds another altar near Bethel.

**Chapter 13**

▲ Abram and his nephew Lot separate. Lot journeys east into the plain of Jordan and settles in Sodom. Abram moves to Hebron and builds another altar to the Lord.

### ◆ God's Third Promise to Abram
God promises the land of Canaan to Abram's offspring.

**Chapter 14**

✳ Nine kings go to war. The victors capture Lot. Abram pursues them and rescues Lot north of Damascus. After rescuing Lot, Abram is blessed by Melchizedek, king of Salem and priest of God Most High.

**Chapter 15**

### ◆ God's Fourth Promise to Abram
God makes a covenant with Abram promising him a multitude of descendants, as numerous as the stars. They will dwell in the land of Canaan after being strangers for 400 years in a foreign land.

**Chapter 16**

✳ Abram's wife Sarai cannot bear children, so she gives her Egyptian slave Hagar to Abram as his wife in order for Abram to have an heir. Hagar becomes pregnant.

✳ Hagar runs away when Sarai deals harshly with her. While in the wilderness, an angel appears to Hagar and tells her to return to Sarai. The angel promises her that her child will have many descendants.

■ Abram and Hagar's son Ishmael is born (2080 BC).

**Chapter 17**

### ◆ God's Fifth Promise to Abram
God reaffirms the covenant he made with Abram, changes Abram's name to Abraham, and Sarai's name to Sarah. God gives Abraham the sign of circumcision which is the mark of God's everlasting covenant.

**Chapter 18**

◆ **God's Sixth Promise to Abraham**
Three visitors remind Abraham that Sarah will bear him a son. Sarah laughs at this because she is so old. God promises them that all nations will be blessed through them and kings will be among their descendants (2067 BC).

**Chapter 19**

✳ God tells Abraham that he will destroy the city of Sodom. Abraham asks God to spare Sodom. God agrees if Abraham can find ten righteous people.

✳ God destroys Sodom and Gomorrah but rescues Lot and his family. Lot's wife becomes a pillar of salt because she looks back at the city. Lot and his daughters escape to the hills.

**Chapter 20**

▲ Abraham travels to Gerar where he tells King Abimelek that his wife Sarah is only his sister.

**Chapter 21**

▆ Isaac is born to Abraham and Sarah (2066 BC).

✳ Sarah requests that Abraham send Hagar and Ishmael away so that Isaac will not have to share his inheritance with Ishmael.

✳ God tells Abraham to send Hagar and Ishmael away. God provides for them and promises to make Ishmael into a great nation.

✳ Ishmael grows up in the wilderness of Paran, marries an Egyptian woman, and becomes an expert archer.

✳ Abraham and Abimelek, the king of Gerar, swear an oath of peace beside a well called Beersheba.

**Chapter 22**

✳ God tests Abraham by commanding him to sacrifice his son Isaac. As Abraham prepares to obey, God stops him and provides a ram as a replacement for Isaac.

◆ **God's Seventh Promise to Abraham**
God again promises Abraham that he will bless him and bless all nations through him. God tells Abraham that his offspring will be as numerous as the stars of heaven and as the sand on the seashore.

▲ Abraham moves to Beersheba.

**Chapter 23**

● Sarah dies at Hebron in the land of Canaan at age 127. She is put to rest in the cave of Machpelah (2029 BC).

**Chapter 24**

✳ Abraham sends his servant to Harran to find Isaac a wife. The servant finds Rebekah and brings her back to Isaac. Rebekah and Isaac are married.

✳ Abraham marries again. His wife Keturah bears him six more sons.

▪ Rebekah gives birth to twins, Jacob and Esau. God tells Rebekah that two nations will come from her womb, one will be stronger, and the elder will serve the younger (2005 BC).

**Chapter 25**

● Abraham dies when he is 175 years old. Isaac and Ishmael bury him in the cave of Machpelah in Hebron with his wife Sarah. Abraham leaves everything he owns to his son Isaac (1991 BC).

✳ Esau sells his birthright (the firstborn's right to the family inheritance) to Jacob for some stew.

**Chapter 26**

▲ Isaac travels to Gerar to escape a famine. Isaac tells King Abimelek and his people that his wife Rebekah is his sister. His trickery is discovered.

◆ **God's First Promise to Isaac**
God tells Isaac not to go to Egypt but to stay in Canaan. God promises Isaac that he will bless him and his descendants with all the land of Canaan. God also tells Isaac that he will make his offspring as numerous as the stars of heaven.

▲ Isaac moves to Beersheba.

✳ Isaac and King Abimelek swear an oath of peace in Beersheba.

◆ **God's Second Promise to Isaac**
While staying in Beersheba, God reaffirms the promise he made to Abraham. Isaac builds an altar to the Lord.

✳ At the age of 40, Esau marries two Hittite women (1965 BC).

● Ishmael dies at age 137 (1943 BC).

**Chapter 27** ✳ Jacob deceives his father Isaac into thinking he is Esau and receives the blessing instead of Esau (1929 BC).

**Chapter 28** ▲ Jacob flees to Harran to escape Esau's anger (1929 BC).

◆ **God's First Promise to Jacob**
On the way to Harran, at Bethel, Jacob has a dream of angels ascending and descending. God reaffirms the promises he made to Abraham and Isaac.

**Chapter 29** ✳ Jacob meets Rachel at Paddan Aram (Harran) and offers her father Laban seven years of service for her hand in marriage (1928 BC).

✳ Laban tricks Jacob and gives him his daughter Leah instead of Rachel, so Jacob agrees to work another seven years for Rachel's hand (1921 BC).

▥ Reuben, the first son of Jacob and Leah, is born.

▥ Simeon, the second son of Jacob and Leah, is born.

▥ Levi, the third son of Jacob and Leah, is born.

▥ Judah, the fourth son of Jacob and Leah, is born.

▥ Dan, the first son of Jacob and Rachel's handmaid Bilhah, is born.

▥ Naphtali, a second son of Jacob and Rachel's handmaid Bilhah, is born.

▥ Gad, the first son of Jacob and Leah's handmaid Zilpah, is born.

▥ Asher, the second son of Jacob and Leah's handmaid Zilpah, is born.

▥ Issachar, the fifth son of Jacob and Leah, is born.

■ Zebulun, the sixth son of Jacob and Leah, is born.

■ Dinah, the daughter of Jacob and Leah, is born.

■ Joseph, the first son of Jacob and Rachel, is born.

**Chapter 30** ✳ Jacob bargains for Laban's livestock and increases in wealth.

**Chapter 31** ▲ Jacob returns to Canaan.

✳ Laban confronts Jacob in Gilead and they make a covenant with each other.

**Chapter 32** ✳ Jacob sends gifts to Esau.

✳ Jacob wrestles with God at Peniel and is renamed Israel ("struggles with God").

**Chapter 33** ✳ Jacob and Esau meet upon Jacob's return.

▲ Jacob settles near Shechem.

**Chapter 34** ✳ Jacob's daughter Dinah is defiled in Shechem and her brothers take revenge.

**Chapters 35–36** ▲ Jacob moves to Bethel.

◆ **God's Second Promise to Jacob**
Jacob builds an altar in Bethel. God appears to Jacob, reaffirms the promise made to Abraham, and again informs Jacob that his name is now Israel.

■ Benjamin, Rachel's second son (Jacob's twelfth son), is born.

● Rachel dies near Bethlehem while giving birth to Benjamin.

▲ Jacob moves to Hebron.

**Chapter 37** ✳ Jacob's favoritism of Joseph, Joseph's ornate coat, and Joseph's dreams cause his brothers to hate him and they plot to kill him.

▲ Joseph is sold by his brothers to Ishmaelite traders on their way to Egypt for 20 pieces of silver. Joseph is sold to Potiphar, Pharaoh's official and captain of the guard (1897 BC). Jacob thinks Joseph is dead.

✳ Joseph is put in charge of Potiphar's household.

**Chapter 38**  ▪ Judah fathers Perez and Zerah, the children of his daughter-in-law Tamar.

**Chapter 39**  ✳ Joseph is imprisoned because of Potiphar's wife's false accusations.

● Isaac dies when he is 180 years old and is buried in Hebron by Esau and Jacob (1886 BC).

**Chapter 40**  ✳ Joseph interprets the dreams of the cupbearer and the baker while in prison.

**Chapter 41**  ✳ Joseph interprets Pharaoh's dreams about seven years of plenty followed by seven years of famine. Pharaoh makes him an official in Egypt (1884 BC).

**Chapter 42**  ✳ Joseph's brothers go to Egypt to buy food during the famine.

✳ Joseph tests his brothers the first time.

**Chapter 43**  ✳ Joseph plans a banquet for his brothers.

**Chapters 44-45**  ✳ Joseph tests his brothers a second time and then reveals his identity to them.

**Chapter 46**  ▲ Jacob's family, now referred to as "Israelites" or "the children of Israel," move to Egypt to live with Joseph and escape the famine (1875 BC). Pharaoh allows them to raise sheep in the land of Goshen (Rameses) and he also puts them in charge of his own livestock.

◆ **God's Third Promise to Jacob**
On the way to Egypt, God appears to Jacob in a vision and promises Jacob that he will make him into a great nation and bring his descendants back to Canaan (the promised land) from Egypt.

**Chapter 47**

✳ Jacob, Joseph's father, meets Pharaoh.

✳ Jacob settles in Goshen. The Israelites gain possessions, are fruitful, and multiply.

**Chapters 48–49**

● Jacob blesses Joseph's sons (Manasseh and Ephraim) and gives them status as tribes of Israel instead of their father. Jacob says his last words to the rest of his sons, and dies at the age of 147. He is buried with Abraham, Sarah, and Isaac in the cave of the field at Machpelah, near Mamre (1859 BC).

**Chapter 50**

✳ After Jacob's death, Joseph tells his brothers that what they intended for evil, God meant for good in order to preserve his people.

● Joseph dies when he is 110 years old (1805 BC). His final request is that his bones be carried to Canaan when God delivers them from Egypt.

▲ During the exodus, Moses takes the bones of Joseph with him. They are buried in Shechem in the promised land of Canaan (Ex. 13:19; Josh. 24:32).

# 10 KEY BIBLE VERSES IN GENESIS

1.  In the beginning God created the heavens and the earth.
    —GENESIS 1:1

2.  And God said, "Let there be light," and there was light.
    —GENESIS 1:3

3.  So God created mankind in his own image, in the image of God he
    created them; male and female he created them. —GENESIS 1:27

4.  Then God blessed the seventh day and made it holy, because
    on it he rested from all the work of creating that he had done.
    —GENESIS 2:3

5.  And I will put enmity between you and the woman, and between
    your offspring and hers; he will crush your head, and you will strike
    his heel. —GENESIS 3:15

6.  The Lord saw how great the wickedness of the human race had
    become on the earth, and that every inclination of the thoughts of
    the human heart was only evil all the time. —GENESIS 6:5

7.  Go from your country, your people and your father's household
    to the land I will show you. I will make you into a great nation,
    and I will bless you; I will make your name great, and you will be a
    blessing. I will bless those who bless you, and whoever curses you
    I will curse; and all peoples on earth will be blessed through you.
    —GENESIS 12:1–3

8.  [Jacob] had a dream in which he saw a stairway resting on the
    earth, with its top reaching to heaven, and the angels of God were
    ascending and descending on it. —GENESIS 28:12

9.  The scepter will not depart from Judah, nor the ruler's staff from
    between his feet, until he to whom it belongs shall come and the
    obedience of the nations shall be his. —GENESIS 49:10

10. You intended to harm me, but God intended it for good to
    accomplish what is now being done, the saving of many lives.
    —GENESIS 50:20

# CHAPTER 2

# The Book of Genesis

**G**enesis is a book of beginnings. In it we read of the origins of the world, of life and death, of good and evil, of God's choice of Abraham and his family to receive blessings and be a blessing, and of God's great plan of redemption. Genesis speaks of creation, the early history of the world, and the ancestors of Israel. Yet Genesis was written not so much to tell us *what* happened as it is a testimony of *why*. The main questions that Genesis addresses are questions of existence and the meaning of life. Who are we? Where did we come from? Why do we exist? Is there purpose to life? Who is God? What is he like? Does he care about people? And what about the human condition, caught in that pervasive cycle where the "heart's gonna do what the heart wants to do"?

The name *Genesis* comes from the Greek word *gignesthai*, which means "to be born" or "to be produced." The Hebrew title of the book is *bereshit*, the first word of the book, which is translated "in the beginning."

## WHY WAS GENESIS WRITTEN?

While Genesis is a book of beginnings, it is also a book of identity: God's and ours. This makes it a book of relationships. We read about many relationships on its pages: between individuals, within families, between shepherds and city-dwellers, with strangers, and especially between people and God. To put it simply, Genesis is a book of real life, sometimes lived redemptively, sometimes lived very much otherwise. And while Genesis focuses on the story of the family of Abraham, it sets the stage for a much longer account of a family, then a people, whom God chose to receive his special revelation so that they might return to life the way it was intended to be at creation. In doing so, the book of Genesis lays the groundwork for understanding:

✠ Why Joshua and the Israelites settled in Canaan;

✠ How Israel became a kingdom, filling their land;

✠ Why the prophets both encouraged and rebuked Israel's behavior in light of God's character and plan for them;

✠ How Israel looked forward to a fulfillment of God's promises—and how these promises were fulfilled in Jesus; and

✠ How believers in Christ continue to live under the blessings, promises, and care of God that were first revealed in Genesis.

In other words, Genesis is the beginning of a long story that continues today and beyond.

## WHO WROTE GENESIS, AND WHEN?

Genesis does not mention the name of its author, nor when it was written. Its title in some English Bible translations, "The First Book of Moses Called Genesis," reflects an early Jewish understanding of Mosaic authorship that developed during the time between the Old and New Testaments. The question as to who wrote Genesis, and when it was written, is actually quite difficult and involves a number of considerations.

Genesis is the first in a group of five books called the Pentateuch: Genesis, Exodus, Leviticus, Numbers, and Deuteronomy. The Pentateuch (from *penta*, meaning "five") is typically labeled "Law"—and understandably so, as these books record not only the narrative of Moses receiving Torah on Mount Sinai but also a very long list (too long for many readers!) of stipulations governing life in ancient Israel.

Some Bible scholars argue that Moses wrote all the books of the Pentateuch. They do so on evidence that the Bible itself seems to indicate this:

✠ Several passages in the Pentateuch state that God told Moses to write about events that happened to Israel on their journey from Egypt to Canaan (Ex. 17:14; 24:4, 7; 34:27; Deut. 31:9, 22, 24).

✠ Other passages in the Bible speak of the "Book of Moses" (Ezra 6:18; Neh. 13:1; Mark 12:26) or the "Book of the Law of Moses" (Josh. 8:31; 23:6; 2 Kings 14:6; Neh. 8:1). (However, scholars who do not accept

Mosaic authorship understand the phrase "the Book of Moses" as indicating a book *about* Moses rather than a book written by him.)

The Pentateuch ends with the narrative of Moses's death. Jewish writers from the time of the New Testament debated whether or not Moses wrote the account of his own death as recorded in Deuteronomy 34:5–21—but this is a very small portion of the Pentateuch.

Some scholars date the life of Moses to the fifteenth century BC, while others say that Moses lived about two hundred years later. In any case, Moses would have written Genesis and the other books of the Pentateuch prior to Israel's entry into Canaan under Joshua.

The Hebrew word *Torah* is commonly translated as "Law," though the root meaning of *Torah* is "direction" and "instruction." These are concepts that emphasize the process of learning *how* to live lives that are whole, redemptive, and fulfilled. This is the essence of another Hebrew word: *shalom*.

Other evidence, however, suggests that Moses did not write all (or possibly any) of the books of the Pentateuch:

- ✠ The Pentateuch itself speaks about earlier books that were used as sources by its author: "The Book of the Wars of the Lᴏʀᴅ" (Num. 21:14) and "The Book of the Covenant" (Ex. 24:7).

- ✠ Some of the poems recorded in the Pentateuch also seem to have been composed earlier, either in written form or more likely spoken or sung. For instance, there is the phrase "This is why the poets say…" in Numbers 21:27, which introduces a poem about the Amorite city of Heshbon, and also the use of the phrase "this is the account of…" to record and organize genealogical material in Genesis.

- ✠ There are several instances of what looks like updating in the Genesis text, such as city names that do not fit the time of the events described in the Pentateuch (see for example, Gen. 14:2, 3, 7, 17).

These and other factors, including differences in genre and literary style, have caused many scholars to argue against the idea that Moses wrote even small portions of the Pentateuch. As a result, the issue of the number and type of sources that the author (or authors) of the Pentateuch may have used, and how long the process of the composition actually took, has occupied scholars for centuries, with many saying that the process lasted well after the return of Israel to the land following the exile in the sixth century BC.

Though we might never know definitively whether Moses actually wrote all or even some of Genesis, the entire Pentateuch makes great sense as the record of the ancestors of Israel—people struggling to understand themselves, God, and their place in the world, and all the while learning what it means to live full, blessed lives under the care and provision of God and recognizing their dependence on him for life itself. For this reason, despite how we might think Genesis and the rest of the Pentateuch were written, these books are the Word of God and lay the theological groundwork for the rest of Scripture.

# GENESIS IN BIBLICAL HISTORY

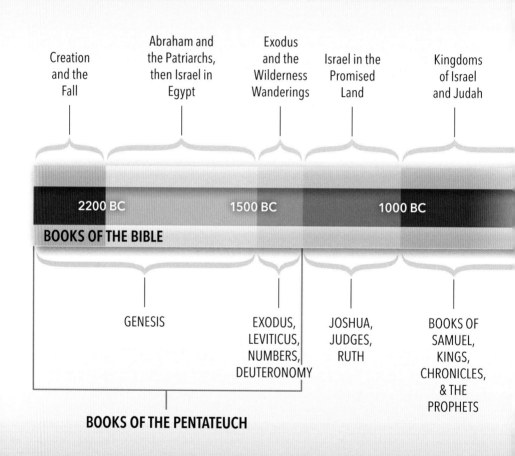

| Creation and the Fall | Abraham and the Patriarchs, then Israel in Egypt | Exodus and the Wilderness Wanderings | Israel in the Promised Land | Kingdoms of Israel and Judah |

2200 BC                    1500 BC                    1000 BC

**BOOKS OF THE BIBLE**

| GENESIS | EXODUS, LEVITICUS, NUMBERS, DEUTERONOMY | JOSHUA, JUDGES, RUTH | BOOKS OF SAMUEL, KINGS, CHRONICLES, & THE PROPHETS |

**BOOKS OF THE PENTATEUCH**

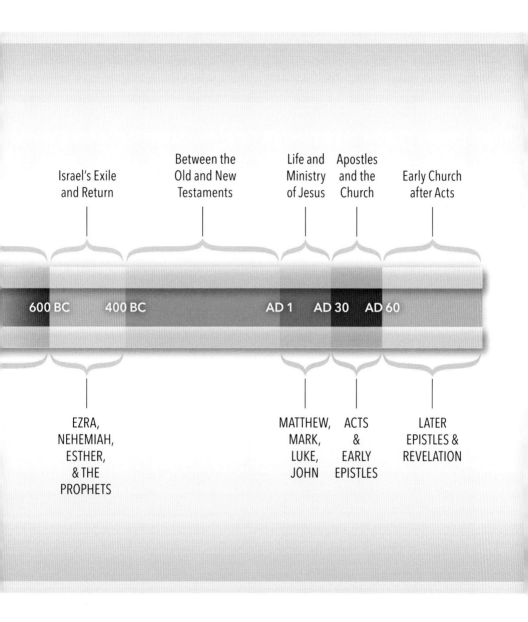

Israel's Exile
and Return

Between the
Old and New
Testaments

Life and
Ministry
of Jesus

Apostles
and the
Church

Early Church
after Acts

600 BC    400 BC          AD 1    AD 30    AD 60

EZRA,
NEHEMIAH,
ESTHER,
& THE
PROPHETS

MATTHEW,
MARK,
LUKE,
JOHN

ACTS
&
EARLY
EPISTLES

LATER
EPISTLES &
REVELATION

# WHAT ARE THE THEMES IN GENESIS?

 ## God as Creator

As Creator, God brings order and life out of disorder and nothingness. The first chapter of Genesis describes the world progressing from a state of being "formless and empty" to that of being "very good," that is, a place fully suitable for people to live (Gen. 1:2; 1:31).

God made people in his own image to live in harmony with the world and with him (Gen. 1:26–27; 5:1; 9:6). Human beings are meant to share some of the same characteristics and roles as their Creator, reflecting his actions and attitudes and caring for each other and everything that he has created. The fact that people are made in the image of God also provides for the dignity and sanctity of human life.

God's rights as the Creator are revealed in the tree of the knowledge of good and evil, the tree from which Adam and Eve were forbidden to eat lest they seize for themselves the right to decide what is and is not good for human life (Gen. 2:9, 16–17). All of this—especially the very natural and enticing temptation to act only for one's own good—plays out in the lives of the families of Adam, Noah, and Abraham as they struggle to respond to God's calling in real-life situations that are, in some respects, not so very different from ours today.

## Covenant

In Genesis, a covenant is a solemn agreement or commitment that binds two parties together for the good of each. Formal covenants could be made between two individuals such as Jacob and Laban (Gen. 31:44–54). More commonly, covenants linked people groups such as families, tribes, cities, or nations, for example Abraham and Isaac to King Abimelek (Gen. 21:22–32; 26:28–30). It is important to note that in the tribal society of Abraham's world, a covenant between individuals always involved others as well, a reminder that the actions of individuals have broad-based consequences.

The Hebrew word for covenant is *berit*, which likely comes from a verb meaning "to bind."

Covenants found in Genesis and throughout the Pentateuch contain elements common to covenants or treaties known from the ancient Near East, such as:

✠ statements listing obligations each party was to perform, often couched in the form of promises;

✠ swearing an oath;

✠ a list of blessings and curses that were conditional based on how the covenant was kept by the parties; and

✠ a list of witnesses to the act of making the covenant; sometimes the witness was a visible sign rather than a person (Gen. 31:51–53).

In Genesis, God's relationship to people is described in terms of a covenant like these, although one initiated by him as the sovereign. Covenants occur at two pivotal places in Genesis and mark significant revelations by God, confirming his desire to provide life, care, and direction for people:

1. The Noahic covenant with the sign of the rainbow (Gen. 6:18; 9:8–17)

2. The Abrahamic covenant with the sign of circumcision (Gen. 15:7–21; 17:1–14)

God renewed the covenant with Abraham's descendants in the form of a promise, or blessing. Many years later, the covenant was expressed by God to Moses at Mount Sinai, the sign being sprinkled blood (Ex. 24:4–8), then to David for an everlasting kingdom (2 Sam. 7:5–16), and eventually to Jeremiah as a new covenant with the sign of a changed heart (Jer. 31:31–34). This new covenant finds its realization in the work of Jesus at the cross and through an international community of believers in him (Luke 22:20; 2 Cor. 3:6).

 ## Promise and Blessing

The theme of promise and blessing is closely related to the theme of covenant. When God blesses someone, or promises to do so, he intervenes in that person's life for well-being (*shalom*) and good (*tov*, the word that describes each day of creation in Genesis 1). Blessings strengthen relationships and anticipate that both the giver and the receiver will live under the benefits of the blessing.

God blessed people at key moments in Genesis. Blessings were given to:

✠ mankind (Adam and Eve) at creation (Gen. 1:27–29; 5:2);

✠ Noah and his sons after the flood (Gen. 9:1–7);

✠ Abraham while living in Harran (Gen. 12:1–3);

✠ Ishmael when Abraham sends him and Hagar away (Gen. 21:13, 18);

✠ Isaac when he goes to Philistine land to escape a famine (Gen. 26:2–5); and

✠ Jacob on multiple occasions (Gen. 28:13–15; 35:11–13; 46:2–4).

God blessed Abraham so that he would be a great *nation* (the Hebrew word is *goy*, which can also be translated "people") and have a great *name* (renowned for his identity with God). This blessing carried the expectation that someday he and his family would also bless others, even those outside his own blood line. This blessing to all peoples was not automatic but rather conditional on their attitude toward Abraham, his family, and his descendants.

I will bless those who bless you, and whoever curses you
I will curse; and all the peoples on earth will be blessed
through you.

GENESIS 12:3

The book of Genesis teaches that God desires to bestow blessings on
everyone, and the family of Abraham was the beginning of the process
by which he would do that. Through receiving God's blessing, Abraham
and his descendants learned
in real time something about
the character of God, as well
as about themselves, living as
they did in a rough-and-tumble
world prone to self-preservation
and intrigue. Genesis also
shows that not everyone chose
to receive God's blessing.
The term *curse* represents a
breakdown of relationships and
an alienation of the parties who
otherwise stood to give and

receive the blessing. When curses occur in Genesis, they reflect a situation
of life that is not the way God intends it to be, and are an explanation for
dysfunction, evil, and death (Gen. 3:14–15, 17–19; 4:11–12; 9:25; 12:3).

Parents in Genesis also bestow blessings on their children or grandchildren:

✠ Bethuel and his wife to their daughter Rebekah (Gen. 24:60)

✠ Isaac to his son Jacob (Gen. 27:27–29)

✠ Isaac to his son Esau (Gen. 27:38–40)

✠ Laban to his daughters Leah and Rachel and to his grandchildren
(Gen. 31:55)

✠ Jacob to his grandchildren Ephraim and Manasseh (Gen. 48:1–20)

✠ Jacob to his sons (Gen. 49:1–28)

This usually happened in the context of a parent transferring rights of authority and use of property to their children. While not all these blessings were equal in terms of what was actually bestowed, each was powerful and had the ability to tangibly alter situations on the ground as well as the mood, attitudes, and actions of the ones receiving the blessing.

## Genealogy

A genealogy is a record of descent from a common ancestor used to determine kinship relationships between people. Organizing family and social relationships through a genealogy was common in the ancient world and remains so in many parts of the world today. Genealogies define identity and belonging within the social structure of a community, society, or culture. People within the same genealogy carry personal and social obligations to provide for and protect each other. The closer one's relationship is to another person in a family tree, the stronger are their rights and responsibilities to ensure that person's good. This is particularly true in societies that are organized around tribal lines, as was much of the ancient Near East in the time of Genesis.

> Though genealogies in ancient times were usually structured around biological ties, a person could also be adopted into a family line.

Tribal society in the world to which Abraham belonged was patriarchal, which meant that descent, rights of inheritance, and land use were traced through the men in the genealogy, with the functional head of the family being the oldest living male. The role of the father was not just to beget children but to provide for and protect those within the genealogy. For this reason, genealogical terms such as *father, mother, son,* and *daughter* became metaphors for other similar relationships, including covenant partners who were otherwise not related by blood, as well as relationships between people and God. The world of Genesis, then, quite naturally gave rise to a depiction of God as father and his people as sons and daughters of God, and also the representation of God as male, emphasizing his role as provider and protector of those under his care.

The story line of Genesis is organized around the phrase "This is the account of." The Hebrew word for account is *toledot,* from a verb meaning "to bear children" (some English Bibles translate the word as "generation"). A *toledot* is a family history and includes not just a genealogical record of succession and who belongs to whom, but an account of important events in the life of the family over several generations. The term occurs eleven times in Genesis, organizing the book into eleven sections of unequal length and content.

| | | |
|---|---|---|
| 1 | "This is the account of the heavens and the earth when they were created." | Genesis 2:4 |
| 2 | "This is the written account of Adam's line." | Genesis 5:1 |
| 3 | "This is the account of Noah." | Genesis 6:9 |
| 4 | "This is the account of Shem, Ham and Japheth, Noah's sons." | Genesis 10:1 |
| 5 | "This is the account of Shem." | Genesis 11:10 |
| 6 | "This is the account of Terah." | Genesis 11:27 |
| 7 | "This is the account of Abraham's son Ishmael." | Genesis 25:12 |
| 8 | "This is the account of Abraham's son Isaac." | Genesis 25:19 |
| 9 | "This is the account of Esau (that is, Edom)." | Genesis 36:1 |
| 10 | "This is the account of Esau the father of the Edomites." | Genesis 36:9 |
| 11 | "This is the account of Jacob." | Genesis 37:2 |

The family accounts recorded in Genesis tell us who the people of these families actually were—their triumphs and downfalls, their victories and struggles, their faithfulness and their sins. These are not random, unconnected stories but purposeful histories about individuals who shaped and revealed God's plan for humanity.

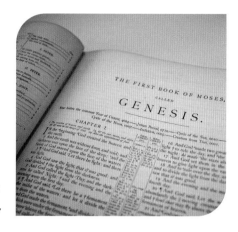

The focus of the book of Genesis narrows down progressively, from interest in the entire universe to interest in one particular family, that of Abraham, and God's call, promise, and covenant with him. Through Abraham's family, God would fix the problem of sin and bring people back to life with him the way it was intended to be at Creation.

## THE *TOLEDOT* OF CREATION

It is interesting that the first *toledot*—account, or generation—is not that of a person or family at all, but of creation, the heavens and earth, the place where people live. By personalizing the heavens and earth this way, the writer of Genesis tells us that all of creation manifests something that is intimate and essential about God. He is the one who brought the world into being (note how Psalm 90:2 speaks of God birthing the world) and has provided for and protected it ever since— and this in spite of the continued actions of people to redefine what it means to be good. By linking creation to the overall story line of Genesis, the writer tells us that creation is not just a one-off event that happened "in the beginning" (Gen. 1:1), but a reminder of the reality in which people live and the hope for a restored creation toward which God's plan of redemption is aimed.

# WHAT IS THE STRUCTURE OF GENESIS?

The book of Genesis can be outlined according to an origin structure in the text.

1.  **Origin of the World:** The Seven Days of Creation (1:1–2:3)

2.  **Origin of the Nations** (2:4–11:9)

    a.  The heavens and the earth (2:4–4:26)

    - Adam and Eve in the Garden of Eden

    - The Fall

    - Cain and Abel

    b.  Adam's line (5:1–6:8)

    - Genealogy from Adam to Noah

    - The Spread of Wickedness across the Earth

    c.  Noah (6:9–9:29)

    - The Flood

    - God's Covenant with Noah

    d.  The Sons of Noah (10:1–11:9)

    - Genealogy of Shem, Ham, and Japheth

    - The Tower of Babel

3.  **Origin of Israel** (11:10–50:26)

    a.  Shem (11:10–26)

    b.  Terah (11:27–25:11)

    - The Call of Abram and His Move to Canaan

    - God's Covenants with Abram (Abraham)

    - Hagar and Ishmael

    - Abraham in Beersheba

    - The Birth, Near-Sacrifice, and Marriage of Isaac

    - The Death of Abraham

    c.  Ishmael (25:12–18)

    d.  Isaac (25:19–35:29)

- Jacob and Esau
- Jacob in Harran with His Wives Leah and Rachel
- Jacob in Canaan

    e.  Esau (36:1–37:1)

    f.  Jacob (37:2–50:26)

- Jacob's Twelve Sons
- Joseph in Egypt
- Jacob and His Family in Egypt

# READING THE BOOK OF GENESIS

As we read through Genesis, it is important to keep in mind a few things about the book.

## 1. Genesis is a historical narrative.

Genesis is an account of real people at real moments in history, who lived in real places (many of which can still be visited). For this reason, Genesis is meant to be read realistically, both in terms of history (what actually happened) and in terms of how people behave (the timeless human condition). The stories of Abraham and his family are accounts of semi-nomadic herders living in semi-arid steppe lands, following seasonal grazing patterns and occasionally coming into contact with people living in more prosperous and settled communities: Egypt, Gerar, Hebron, Shechem, and Harran. Life in this context was difficult, with risks of many kinds, and through it we are able to see how Abraham's family struggled to find security and a future in very practical ways, though not always following the voice of God in the process.

## 2. Genesis is also great literature.

Here we have all the elements of a magnificent story, with the development of plot and subplots; rising and falling action, suspense, crisis, and resolution; precise dialogue and the voice of the narrator; and the actions and voice of God. For most of the Genesis story line, God acts behind the scenes, fronting himself at key moments to keep the actions and attitudes of the other characters on track (they sometimes listen), but clearly he is someone who is in control of the ultimate outcome.

## 3. Most importantly, Genesis is inspired Scripture.

The book of Genesis is a revelation about God. In showing us who God is, the book also reveals who human beings are, using the account of specific individuals and their developing relationship with God to do so. This prompts us, the readers of Genesis, to ask, "Where am *I* in the narrative? How am I like Cain or Abel, Abraham or Sarah, Isaac or Rebekah, Jacob or Esau, or even pharaoh or King Abimelek? How should I think of God

in the situations in which I am living?" If we try—and are honest in the attempt—it is not hard to see ourselves in the characters of Genesis, even the scoundrels. To see their attitudes and actions helps us better see and understand our own.

Because Genesis is inspired Scripture, it is a book of instruction, *torah*, teaching us how to respond to God, the Creator who cares. It also teaches us how to respond to people—

not all of whom are friendly—in ways that are proper, helpful, and consistent with our Creator's desire for our lives. But as inspired Scripture, Genesis also points to Jesus, the scepter of Judah (Gen. 49:10) who will "crush [the] head" of evil (Gen. 3:15). Genesis is not just a book of history, great literature, and instruction for life, it is also special revelation, showing us the need for a Savior and pointing his way.

# CHAPTER 3

# Understanding the World of Genesis

Within the pages of Genesis, we meet the patriarchs and matriarchs of faith—people with names like Abraham, Sarah, Isaac, Rebekah, Jacob, Rachel, Leah, and Joseph. Their names and stories may be quite familiar to us today, but their world and daily lives could not have been more different. It is far too easy to read these beloved stories in Genesis and interpret them through our own place, culture, and language—often

Ruins in Mardin, Turkey
(ancient Mesopotamia)

without even recognizing we are doing so. Take, for example, the names in our English Bibles. If we were to travel back in time and call out to "Jacob" instead of "Ya'akov" in a crowded marketplace, he would not have turned around to answer. If such differences are found in the mere pronunciation of names, how much more might we discover about the stories in Genesis by reading them with a deeper understanding of the geography, culture, and daily life rhythms of the patriarchs and matriarchs.

| ANCIENT EASTERN WORLDVIEW | MODERN WESTERN WORLDVIEW |
| --- | --- |
| The world is static, stable. | The world is always changing. |
| Agricultural/livestock | Industrial |
| Values land, place, tradition | Values exploration, travel, independence |
| Limited resources | Limitless resources |
| Household/community centered | Individual centered |
| Elderly are wise, highly esteemed. | Elderly are burdens, out of touch. |
| Youth are foolish. | Youth are cutting edge. |
| Patriarchal, patrilineal, patrilocal | Egalitarian |
| Story centered | History/facts centered |
| Everything is religious; there are no atheists. | There is separation between sacred and secular. |

# FROM EMPIRE TO A LAND BETWEEN

Where are you right now? Where were you born and where do you live? Those of us who live close to nature, in forests and on farmlands, experience daily rhythms differently than those of us who live in urban landscapes. Multicultural places where the world intersects, with many visitors and immigrants, differ from communities that are more remote, established, and culturally similar. A seemingly mundane detail such as "place of birth" follows us through our lives, shaping our national, cultural, ethnic, and religious identities. When meeting a new friend or colleague, we often ask, "Where are you from?" or "Where did you grow up?" It is not just data we seek, but this knowledge helps us understand one another.

Our place in this world shapes our view of the world—and also how we think about God and our relation to him. The same was true for those in the world of Genesis.

## Mesopotamia and Egypt

What was Abraham's homeland like? Originally from Ur of the Chaldeans (Gen. 11:28), on the eastern edge of the Fertile Crescent, Abraham and Sarah move from the dominating international power of Mesopotamia to the modest land of Canaan.

Nile River, Egypt

The name *Mesopotamia* describes its very location: *meso* means "between" or "in the middle," and *potamos* means "river." Situated in the valleys between the mighty Euphrates and Tigris Rivers, Abraham's home was located in a vibrant and sophisticated civilization. The rivers provided fresh water, mineral-rich soil, and abundant crops, creating a fertile place for the birth of the Mesopotamian empire, bringing about wealth, resources, and international trade.

At the southwestern end of the Fertile Crescent, the Egyptian empire ruled from the banks of the lush, green Nile River. This northward flowing river provided abundant crops, trade, transportation, and fresh water, serving as a trusted haven for the surrounding nations during famines. Abraham (and later Jacob) sought survival in Egypt during times of drought and famine but was warned not to remain there. (Indeed, by the first chapter of Exodus, we see that the Israelites ultimately become enslaved in the power hungry empire of Egypt.)

## The Land of Canaan

Between the two powers of Mesopotamia and Egypt was the land of Canaan. This is the land that God called the patriarchs and matriarchs of Genesis to. But why *this* land? Canaan, quite literally meaning a "land between" and later known as Israel, was situated between powers and empires to the north and the south.[1] Stuck between the mighty Mediterranean Sea to the west and a massive desert to the east, the land served as a "sacred bridge" in the ancient Near East.[2]

The land was very small, yet the terrain drastically changes within very close quarters. Made up of a sandy coastal plain, lowlands and foothills, fertile valleys, tight mountainous regions, from the snow-capped heights of Hermon to desolate deserts, Canaan contained all the environmental and geographical diversity found in the state of California within an area smaller than New Jersey. When we read the stories in Genesis, the place and time of year greatly inform the situation in which the patriarchs find themselves.

Mt. Hermon and valley below

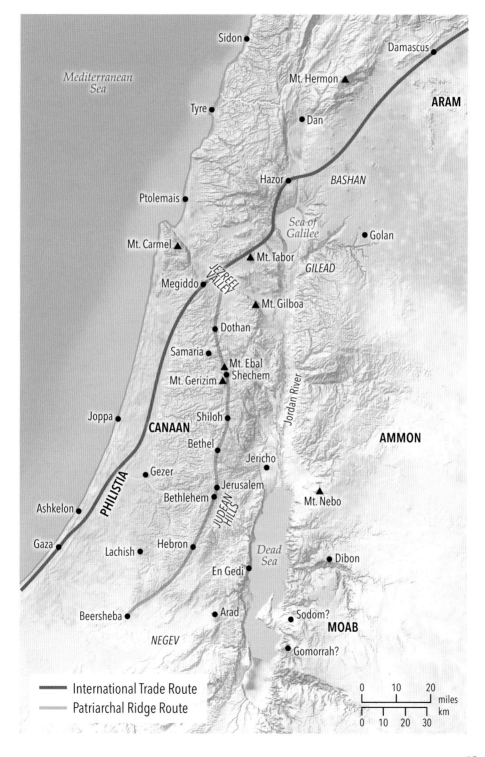

Mediterranean
Sea

Sidon

Damascus

Mt. Hermon ▲

ARAM

Tyre

Dan

Hazor

BASHAN

Ptolemais

Sea of
Galilee

Golan

Mt. Carmel ▲

▲ Mt. Tabor

GILEAD

JEZREEL
VALLEY

Megiddo

▲ Mt. Gilboa

Dothan

Samaria

▲ Mt. Ebal
Shechem
Mt. Gerizim ▲

Jordan River

Joppa

Shiloh

CANAAN

Bethel

AMMON

Jericho

Gezer

Jerusalem

PHILISTIA

Bethlehem

▲ Mt. Nebo

Ashkelon

JUDEAN
HILLS

Gaza

Hebron

Dead
Sea

Lachish

Dibon

En Gedi

Beersheba

Arad

Sodom?

MOAB

NEGEV

Gomorrah?

International Trade Route
Patriarchal Ridge Route

0        10        20
|----|----|----|----| miles
                        km
0    10    20    30

Compared to the expansive kingdoms of Mesopotamia and Egypt, the biblical land of Canaan was incredibly small and compact. The boundaries of the land vary depending on the historical period. The distance between Dan and Beersheba, the traditional northern and southern boundaries, was only 150 miles (240 km). Abraham traveled this distance and more to rescue of Lot, passing through the mud brick Canaanite gate at Tel Dan on his way toward Damascus (Gen. 14).

Tel Dan Canaanite gate

The dramatic elevations in the land affect climate, habitation, and ease of travel.

- ✠ Mount Hermon is 9,200 feet high (2,800 m), while only 25 miles south (40 km), the Sea of Galilee is 685 feet (209 m) *below* sea level.

- ✠ Jerusalem is 2,593 feet (790 m) *above* sea level while only 15 miles (24 km) east, the Dead Sea is 1,275 feet (389 m) *below* sea level, the lowest place on earth.

Given these significant altitude differences in such tight quarters, it is possible to experience wintery snow or rain in Jerusalem, while gazing to the east at sunny skies in places like Jericho, only 15 miles (24 km) away.

During the rainy season, the Jordan River may flood its banks as water rushes southward, but the mighty Jordan is nothing compared the Tigris and Euphrates Rivers of Mesopotamia or the Nile River in Egypt. The Jordan flows from the base of Mount Hermon to fill the freshwater Sea of Galilee, the northern harp-shaped body of water (Num. 34:11). In Hebrew, the word Jordan (*yarden*) means "to go down." People in the ancient world understood geography and named this river in light of the massive elevation changes from the Jordan headwaters near Mount Hermon to the below-sea-level Galilee.

The Jordan River flows south in a winding fashion for about 65 miles (105 km) to the Dead Sea, where it ends. Jacob crossed this river on his return to Canaan (Gen. 32:10). This area may have looked to the ancient peoples enticing from a distance, but it lacked the sloping river banks and fertile soil necessary to create agricultural land or trade routes for either goods or people.

Upon hearing the word *sea* in "Sea of Galilee," many of us picture a large expanse of water with crashing surf. However, the Sea of Galilee is a small freshwater lake only about 13 miles (21 km) in length and 6.8 miles (11 km) at its widest point.

The Judean hills, on the other hand, were made of limestone and were characterized by steep slopes and very fertile soil, making this area excellent for growing fruit trees and vines in terraced hillsides. A north-south trade route ran along the eastern edge of the Judean hills. This trade route is commonly called the Patriarchal Ridge Route, because it was frequently traveled by the patriarchs when visiting Bethel and Hebron (Gen. 12:8; 13:18; 23:19; 35:6–7, 27). The route also served as a dividing line between the wet west and dry east. The moisture from the Mediterranean rises up from the sea, providing rain for the lowlands and the Judean hills, but once it moves past the ridge route to the Judean wilderness, the rugged terrain falls in the rainshadow, with the chalky limestone shedding off any water toward the Dead Sea.

Jordan River flowing to the Dead Sea

As one moves south along that ridge route, the Judean hills fade away and the Negev comes into view. Abraham, Isaac, and Jacob spent much of their time in places like Beersheba in the Negev (Gen. 21:33–34, 22:19; 26:23–25; 46:1). About fifteen miles (24 km) north of Beersheba marks the northern border of the Negev, the "dryland" stretching toward the south.

## The International Trade Route

The International Trade Route ran along the coastal plain, parallel to the Mediterranean Sea, connecting Egypt with the kingdoms to the north and east. There were three north-south trade routes in the land, but the coastal plain provided the greatest ease for travel, trade, and communication. It connected in the north with the Jezreel Valley, the most important east-west crossing in Canaan.

Combined with rich soil, the abundance of springs, and high ground-water level, the coastal plain was the richest and most populated region of Canaan. This region and trade route was subject to frequent contests and interaction with foreign neighbors. Control of this route meant safety for travelers and the transport of goods, which brought about wealth through taxation. Merchants and armies could travel by foot upwards of 20 miles (32 km) a day on these well-worn routes, making Canaan a highly sought-after region, regularly conquered, and utilized by the surrounding empires—or, as Bible lands scholar Paul Wright has called it, "a land of mice where cats come to play."[3]

Jezreel Valley

This region functioned much like a bridge, connecting the three continents of Europe, Asia, and Africa. Anyone wanting to avoid travel by desert or by sea had to pass through Canaan. Abraham's family and their descendants settled in an intersecting place, as the world passed through on their way to empires, resources, trade, wealth, and power. As the people of the world traversed through this "land between," the people of God did not have to go anywhere in order to fulfill the words of the Lord: All families on earth would be blessed through Abraham and his descendants (Gen. 12:3).

## THE GEZER CALENDAR

The Gezer calendar is a Canaanite inscription on a small limestone tablet dating to the tenth century BC discovered in 1908. Found just 20 miles (32 km) west of Jerusalem, the inscription details the annual agricultural cycle in Canaan. Interestingly, the calendar corresponds with the biblical harvest and festival calendar of the ancient Israelites (Lev. 23).

The sowing of grains started after the first rains, around November/December. The barley harvest was first, around March/April, and the wheat, planted just a bit later, was harvested in May/June. The harvest of summer fruits occurred around August/September. There was always work to be done in the land and never a season of rest, with various crops coming to fruition at different times in the year.

Gezer calendar reads:

- ✠ two months of ingathering [olives]

- ✠ two months of sowing [cereals]

- ✠ two months of late sowing [legumes and vegetables]

- ✠ a month of hoeing weeds [for hay]

- ✠ a month of harvesting barley

- ✠ a month of harvesting [wheat] and measuring [grain]

- ✠ two months of grape harvesting

- ✠ a month of ingathering summer fruit

# A GOOD LAND

The author of Deuteronomy describes the land of Canaan as a good land, flowing with water. It was a land where water could be found in fresh springs, aquifers, wells, and rivers. It was also a land of "milk and honey," providing a place for both shepherds and farmers with enough land for both grazing and agriculture, without conflict, a land where people could eat and be satisfied.

## The Seven Species

The land of Canaan was one of "wheat and barley, vines and fig trees and pomegranates, a land of olive oil and honey" (Deut. 8:8). This agricultural promise of these seven species became symbolic of God's provision for the people. (The "honey" was likely the sweet jam of the date palm.) Unlike their southern and eastern neighbors, the terraced hillsides of the Judean mountains and the green valleys in Galilee made cultivation of these fruit trees, vines, and olive trees possible. The seven species appear frequently throughout the biblical text, illuminating aspects of daily life, religious life, and trade.

| SPECIES | | SYMBOLIZES | EXAMPLE |
|---|---|---|---|
| | 1. Wheat grains<br>2. Barley grains | Blessing, harvest, and provision | Gen. 27:28 |
| | 3. Grape vine | Israel | Isa. 5 |
| | 4. Fig tree | Leadership and security | 1 Kings 4:25 |
| | 5. Pomegranate | Fertility | Song 7:12 |
| | 6. Olive tree | Light | Ex. 27:20 |
| | 7. Date palm | Righteousness | Ps. 92:12 |

# Rain in Its Season

Genesis marks two seasons: wet and dry. They are also referred to as "seedtime and harvest," "cold and heat," or "winter and summer" (Gen. 8:22). With a short rainy season (October to April), rainfall in the northernmost parts of Israel could be as much as 44 inches, while in the southern Negev, only 3 to 5 inches.

Rainfall varies year to year, and droughts are frequent in the Negev. This reality impacted the seasonal rhythms of the people living in the time of Genesis. Just the little bit of annual rainfall could sustain small crops of barley and wheat. These were essential crops for the desert dwellers, making up 80 percent of their meager diet, and the grinding of these grains was a daily household task for the women.[4] No wonder Isaac rejoiced when he "reaped a hundredfold" when the Lord blessed him (Gen. 26:12).

Olive oil was used for a variety of purposes in the ancient Near East: anointing (Gen. 28:18; Ex. 30:25), lighting lamps (Ex. 27:20), cooking (Ex. 29:2), cosmetics (Ps. 104:15), medicines (Isa. 1:6), and trade (Hos. 12:1; 1 Kings 5:11).

As rain falls miles away in the Judean hills, dry wadis in the Negev can suddenly fill with fast moving waters rushing through, taking along anything in their path. Still today, drowning is one of the primary causes of death in the Judean wilderness and Negev, as people are caught unaware in these fast-moving waters. Psalm 23 reflects this danger as the psalmist longs for the calm, safe waters only the shepherd can provide: "The LORD is my Shepherd.... He leads me beside the still waters" (verses 1–2). When storms come, wise shepherds know to stay on the high ground, on the rock, avoiding the sandy wadis below.

Most of these floods flow into the Mediterranean or the Dead Sea, but along their way, they fill the springs and wells of the Negev, providing water during the dry seasons. In Scripture, water in the Negev is a sign of divine favor, a blessing that causes the desert to bloom: "[The Lord] turned the desert into pools of water and the parched ground into flowing springs" (Ps. 107:35; see also Ps. 126:4; Isa. 35:1; 43:20).

Rainfall, living water, was seen as a supernatural gift from God, given as a reward for obedience of the people.

> The eyes of the LORD your God are always upon [this land], from the beginning of the year to the end of the year … giving the rain for your land in its season, the early rain and the later rain, that you may gather in your grain and your wine and your oil.
>
> DEUTERONOMY 11:12, 14 ESV

Unlike Mesopotamia and Egypt with their large freshwater rivers, where people "planted … seed and irrigated it by foot" (Deut. 11:10), survival in Canaan depended completely on annual rainfall. When the rainfall was abundant, more crops could be planted yielding a greater harvest. Hillside grazing pastures supported larger flocks of livestock, bringing more resources for the community and less conflict. Longer wet seasons provided abundant streams and springs, filling up wells and cisterns. But in years of drought, when the eastern desert crept closer toward the Judean mountains, water sources dried up, crops withered, flocks died, and famine took hold in the land.

When Genesis speaks of famine, we must realize that this was not simply a shortage of food. It was a shortage of everything necessary for life. A drought meant no agriculture, for both humans and animals. As the animals went hungry and thirsty, their ability to procreate and feed their

Judean Hills

own young was also lost. Within just one or two seasons of drought, families would lose between 20 to 40 percent of their flock. With no animals left to provide dairy, meat, fleece, hair, clothing, blankets or tents, the people would suffer from thirst, hunger, and cold.

In Genesis 37, Joseph is sent by his father Jacob to check on his brothers who are shepherding the flocks. Joseph finds them in Dothan, near the Jezreel Valley. They are in the northwest, far from the more common locales of Hebron

Joseph's Well, Dothan (photo c. 1950)

and Beersheba because they are desperately looking for pasture for their flocks. Notice that when they throw Joseph into the cistern, it is empty (Gen. 37:24). A severe drought is beginning, and it will bring with it famine throughout the region. The brothers happen to be on the eastern fork of the International Trade Route. Joseph is sold into slavery along this trade route leading south to Egypt. Parental favoritism, braggadocious behavior, and sibling rivalry provide a colorful backdrop to the story, but famine is foreshadowed through the geography and climate. Later in the story, Joseph will rise within the ranks of Egypt with its great Nile River in order to store up grain for the coming calamity. The survival of Jacob's family becomes dependent upon this turn of events.

Many people today live in places with easy access to daily resources. If we want water, we simply turn on a tap. If we want food, we go to a grocery store; fresh produce and meats, local and imported from various parts of the world, await us there. The people of Genesis, however, did not live in a time of such ease. Even the most privileged and wealthy among them knew the fragility of life in the land, subject to the rhythms of the wet and dry seasons, negotiating and conserving every drop of water and every precious resource. All peoples of the ancient Near East practiced the values of "reduce, reuse, recycle" without any public service announcement. From season to season, they lived on the edge of survival, fluctuating between times of scarcity and abundance.

# THE RHYTHMS OF DAILY LIFE

In the ancient world of Genesis, even during years with much rainfall, maintaining a nomadic lifestyle was essential to survival during the long dry seasons. The more barren, desert regions, like the boundary areas of the southern Judean mountains and the Negev, could not support large agricultural crops, and there was never enough pastureland to sustain a flock settled in one place for too long.

Caring for livestock was vital for our nomadic ancestors.

✠ The sons of Jacob are introduced to Pharaoh as shepherds, keepers of livestock, just like their ancestors (Gen. 46:31–34).

✠ Abraham sent his servant with camels on his mission to find a wife for his son Isaac (Gen. 24:10).

Goats, sheep, and camels provided dairy, wool, hair, and occasionally meat, for the families. Flocks were primarily female. A few males were kept for husbandry but were otherwise used mostly for sale or slaughter (Gen. 32:14–15).

Flocks could not graze just anywhere. Nomadic flocks were a threat to sown fields (Num. 20:18–20). Conflict occurred between shepherds and farmers, between the migrants and the settled. But in this land of milk and honey, there was a place for all, and ways to work together. After the fall harvest, flocks grazed on the remaining stubble in the fields, providing essential fertilizing before the wet season and planting began. During the wet season, shepherds led their flocks through the Judean wilderness and Negev, from one patch of pasture to another, finding water from pooling rainfall and moist grasses.

The sheep and goats we read about in Genesis would have required four gallons of water a day, while camels needed eleven to sixteen gallons every two or three days.

Once the hot, dry season came in late spring, families encamped close to wells and springs. Abraham and his descendants, following this rhythm, spent the dry season at the well near the oaks of Mamre in Hebron (Gen. 18) and the wet season in the western Negev (Gen. 20).

The patriarchs and matriarchs could easily spend entire days on foot as households moved about the land. Depending on the heat and terrain, families with flocks and possessions covered approximately six to eight miles (10–13 km) a day, carrying their water in skins and seeking resources along the way. Intimate knowledge of the land was passed down from generation to generation, sharing the places and names of water sources, herbs, plants, and grazing regions. They traveled light, with only essential household possessions. Easy-to-move tents allowed them to move from place to place as needed. Tent poles were likely made of acacia trees and the tent itself made of goat hair (similar to the tabernacle in Exodus 25:4, 13; 35:26). Goat hair soaks up rainwater, drawing tighter during a storm, keeping everyone within the tents warm and dry.

With flocks and herds as their source of wealth and security, the ancient Israelites primarily ate grain, along with some dairy products, and the very occasional bird, goat, or sheep as a source of protein. Thin, unleavened bread made of flour and water was cooked over an open fire in ashes or on top of a thin metal disk called a taboon. Soft when hot and hard like a cracker when cooled, this bread was often served with some hard cheese or a bit of oil and herbs. When flocks were nursing, buttermilk and butter was churned in a skin for a special treat.

This nomadic lifestyle meant everyone would at some point find themselves as strangers in a strange land, vulnerable and dependent upon the generosity of others to survive. Hospitality was indispensable within

the desert culture. In Genesis 18, Abraham is sitting at the entrance to his tent in the heat of the day. He is by the great trees of Mamre near Hebron. As he looks up, he sees three men standing nearby and hurries to greet them, bowing low to them and begging them to enter his tent. Water is brought, feet are washed, Sarah prepares bread of the finest flour, and a choice calf is sacrificed. If we were sitting on our front porch today, this would not be our first impulse upon noticing three strange men on our street. And yet, nothing was more natural for Abraham. Desert hospitality dictated that anyone must be welcomed into a tent for up to three days, no questions asked.

Today, there is a welcoming saying in Israel: "All four sides of my tent are open." This is based upon a rabbinic tradition that Abraham opened all four sides of his tent to receive those passing by.

In contrast to Abraham's welcome, we see the wickedness and cruelty toward the vulnerable strangers in Sodom in Genesis 19. Abraham's nephew Lot risks his very life, and the lives of his daughters, in order to ensure the safety of his guests.

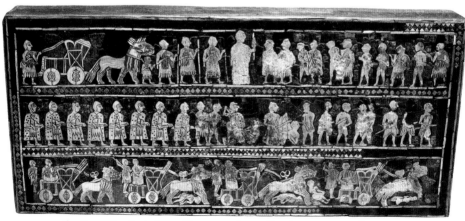

The Royal Standard of Ur, a Mesopotamian artifact dating to around 2600 BC, shows scenes of war, peace, and daily life.

# THE FATHER'S HOUSE

Residing in a land with no centralized government or legal system, desert culture and customs, like the practice of hospitality, provided safety, structure, and justice for the tribe. It was necessary for shepherds, often both girls and boys, to lead their flocks to various grazing areas, some distance away from the encampment. Shepherding could be difficult and

dangerous (Gen. 31:39–40). In a world where many of us hesitate to let our children walk a few blocks to school, it is hard to imagine sending off children to shepherd flocks on their own, well out of sight.

Unique to the culture of these nomadic desert dwellers was the concept of the "father's house," or the *beit-av.* The members of one's tribe and household were under the protection of the father, even when far from home. If any harm came to their children or their flock, justice would come swiftly: eye for eye, tooth for tooth, life for life. Tribal wars broke out, camps were raided, and destruction came swiftly upon any responsible.

## REBEKAH'S DECISION

Women in the ancient world rarely negotiated on their own behalf or were given any say in decisions to marry. Rebekah is the noticeable exception. In Genesis 24:28, she refers to her mother's house, the *beit-im*, as opposed to her father's house. When she is called to leave everything she has ever known to marry Isaac in Canaan, her mother and brother ask her whether she will agree to go (Gen. 24:58). Rebekah courageously answers yes, receives her blessing, and becomes the love of Isaac's life and the mother of Jacob and Esau.

When we first meet Abraham in Genesis, God calls him to leave everything he has known—his identity, his family, his place—to follow a God he cannot see to a land not yet known.

> Now the LORD said to Abram, "Go from your country and your kindred and your father's house to the land that I will show you."

GENESIS 12:1

God tells Abraham to leave his "father's house" (*beit-av*). This seemingly poetic term carried much weight within the context of the ancient world. The father's house was not a building or place but referred to the governing tribal structure by which the people of Genesis lived.[5] The father's house provided a system of belonging, identity, protection, and provision. People who lacked a father's house, like widows, orphans, and strangers, lacked this system. Abraham knows he and his loved ones will be leaving that all behind.

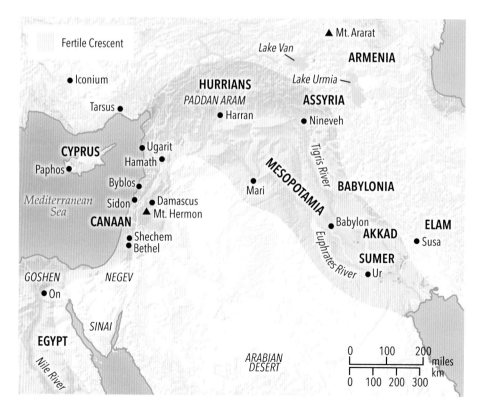

After arriving in Canaan, Abraham once again departs; this time for Egypt to escape a famine.

> When he was about to enter Egypt, he said to his wife Sarai, "I know well that you are a woman beautiful in appearance, and when the Egyptians see you, they will say, 'This is his wife'; they will kill me, but they will let you live. Say you are my sister, so that it may go well with me because of you and that my life may be spared on your account."
>
> GENESIS 12:11–13

When we read this story, especially through the lens of our modern worldview, it is easy to be shocked and wonder: How can Abraham be characterized as a father and hero of the faith when he lacked the courage and moral fortitude required to protect his wife? In fact, Abraham lied about his wife's identity on two occasions (Gen. 12; 20). When confronted with his lie, Abraham explained the reason for this deception: "I said to myself, 'There is surely no fear of God in this place, and they will kill me because of my wife" (Gen. 20:11). In their cultural context, both Abraham and Sarah are displaced and without protection. When Abraham takes on the role of Sarah's brother, he is now the head of her *beit-av,* and as such, is seen as her protector and avenger. He must be negotiated with and respected, for the sake of peace. In the culture of the ancient Near East, this was the norm.

It is no wonder that the books of Exodus, Leviticus, and Deuteronomy repeatedly instruct the Israelites to care for and protect the most vulnerable: the stranger, orphan, and widow. In ancient Israelite culture, the most vulnerable were under the protection and authority of God himself, members of God's *beit-av.*

This cultural key unlocks much of Genesis, as well as the larger biblical narrative, even reaching into the life and teachings of Jesus.

- ✠ When Jesus's parents locate him in God's temple, a twelve-year-old Jesus tells them, "Did you not know I would be in my Father's house?" (Luke 2:49).

- ✠ Jesus taught his disciples that "in my father's house, there are many rooms" (John 14:2).

In Christ, believers are no longer orphans or strangers but are called friends and children of God.

In Genesis, it is not Abraham's birthplace or his father's religion and authority that define him but his departure from everything familiar. Deuteronomy 26:5 gives voice to this new reality. When observing the feast of firstfruits, Israel was to come before the Lord and declare: "My father was a wandering Aramean." It is Abraham's wandering that becomes his identity and heroic characteristic. This statement is a remembrance of Abraham's courage to leave everything and trust a God he could not see, wandering to a land unknown.

For those of us who have also had to leave behind place, family, security, and stability, we can find hopeful examples in Abraham and other patriarchs and matriarchs in Genesis. We are invited to trust that in our wanderings, God is our Father, and we belong to his *beit-av*.

## Notes

1. The term *Land Between* was first used by Dr. James Monson to refer to the land of biblical Israel.

2. *The Sacred Bridge* by Anson F. Rainey and Steven Notley (Carta 2015).

3. *Holman Illustrated Guide to Biblical Geography: Reading the Land* by Paul H. Wright (Holman 2020), 63.

4. *Bedouin Culture in the Bible* by Bailey Clinton (Yale University Press 2018), 30.

5. *Epic of Eden: A Christian Entry into the Old Testament* by Sandra Richter (IVP Academic 2008), 27.

# CHAPTER 4

# Noah's Ark

The story of Noah's ark is so well popularized that even people who may have never read the story in the book of Genesis feel like they know it already. But what for many has become a cute children's tale is, in the Bible, a pivotal narrative revealing something fundamental about the nature of God and people.

While details and debates surrounding the extent of the flood, the size of the ark, and the kinds of animals on board are all worth considering, these are not the narrative's primary message. Rather, the reason for the story can be seen in enduring themes that link it to other parts of the book of Genesis, as well as to the entire Bible. It is difficult to treat the story of Noah's ark as a stand-alone account and grasp the full impact of the consequences of the flood, God's means of salvation, and our response.

## THE ACCOUNT OF NOAH

The narrative opens with these words: "The account of Noah ..." (Gen. 6:9). This *account* fills about one third of the history of Genesis before Abraham is introduced in chapter 11.

Although Genesis provides many details about the flood and the ark, much is left unsaid or remains open to interpretation.

## THE ARK (Gen. 6:9–22)

Now the earth was corrupt in God's sight and was full of violence.... So God said to Noah, "I am going to put an end to all people, for the earth is filled with violence because of them. I am surely going to destroy both them and the earth. So make yourself an ark."

GENESIS 6:11, 13

The biblical text says that God told Noah about his plans to flood the earth and instructed Noah to build an ark to save him and his family, but it does not say when Noah began to build the ark, how he gained the necessary engineering expertise to do so, who helped him, how he could afford to build it, or how long it took. The popular suggestions that Noah was ridiculed by his neighbors and that he spent time warning the peoples of the world about God's upcoming judgment appear only in much later Jewish and Christian texts (Josephus, Jubilees, and the writings of Augustine; Peter calls Noah "a preacher of righteousness;" 2 Peter 2:5).

The Hebrew word for ark is *tevah*. It is actually an Egyptian word that means "chest." The only other use of this word in the Bible is for the vessel into which the infant Moses was placed. (The word for ark of the covenant is a different term: *'aron*). Noah's ark was made of *gopher* wood, a Hebrew term that may indicate either cypress or oak. The joints were sealed with pitch "inside and out" (Gen. 6:14).

The dimensions of the ark are given in Hebrew in cubits, a unit of length that varied in the ancient world but was about 18 inches (46 cm). The ark's overall dimensions were a ratio of 6:1, considered to be a stable vessel today. The size of the ark was significantly larger than any other known vessel of the ancient world, or for that matter, any boat until the late nineteenth century AD. Estimates about the number of animals that the ark could hold are as high as 50,000.

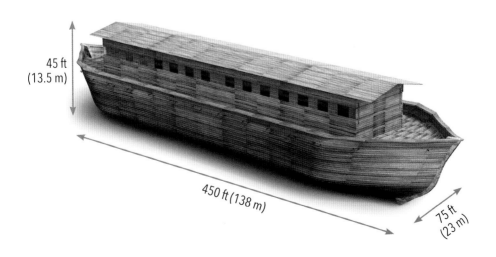

45 ft (13.5 m)

450 ft (138 m)

75 ft (23 m)

Make a roof for it, leaving below the roof an opening one cubit high all around. Put a door in the side of the ark and make lower, middle and upper decks.

GENESIS 6:16

Genesis 6:16, a difficult verse to translate, is usually understood as indicating that the ark had three decks containing rooms, a single door in the hull, and a row of relatively small windows just under the roofline. A wide variety of reconstructions of the ark have been made over the years, both actually and in art.

Life-sized reconstruction of Noah's ark ("The Ark Encounter" in Williamstown, Kentucky)

## THE ANIMALS (Gen. 7:1–9)

Take with you seven pairs of every kind of clean animal, a male and its mate, and one pair of every kind of unclean animal, a male and its mate.

GENESIS 7:2

Noah, his family, two pairs of every unclean animal and seven pairs of every clean animal enter the ark. According to Leviticus 11, clean animals are those suitable for sacrifice and human consumption. The animals on the ark were "of every kind" (Gen. 6:19, 20). We do not know if *kind* refers to species or a different category (Gen. 1:21, 24). There is also no indication as to the actual process by which the animals "came to Noah" (Gen. 6:20; 7:8, 15); how the animals were kept healthy, other than that they were fed (Gen. 6:21); how they were kept docile, especially the non-domesticated ones (Gen. 7:14); what the ages of the animals were; or if any reproduced or perished during the journey. It is also interesting that nothing is said about fish, even though a massive flood would have wreaked havoc with saltwater and freshwater habitats.

## THE FLOOD (Gen. 7:10–24)

The waters rose and increased greatly on the earth, and the ark floated on the surface of the water. They rose greatly on the earth, and all the high mountains under the entire heavens were covered.

GENESIS 7:18–19

After waiting seven days, the rains fell for forty days and forty nights. The flood covered the earth for 150 days. The flood started when "the springs of the great deep burst forth and the floodgates of the heavens were opened" (Gen. 7:11). It is possible to explain the presence of subterranean waters sufficient for a flood that covered the highest mountains on earth to a depth of 20 feet (6 m) only if we assume a very different geological structure prior to the flood (Gen. 7:20).

One question that has led to considerable debate is about the extent of the flood: Did the floodwaters cover the entire earth or only a local region where Noah lived? While it is possible that certain geological features of the earth today were caused by a massive flood in ancient times, many portions of the globe show no evidence of significant flooding. In any case, arguments for a universal flood are strongest if the existence of current geological structures cannot be explained by any other means.

Some cities in Mesopotamia, the likely location of Noah's home, show archaeological evidence of having been inundated by a flood (for example, Ur, Uruk, Shuruppak, Lagash, Kish, and Nineveh), though at different times (the fourth and third millennia BC). Most ancient cities in the area, however, reveal no indication of having been flooded, even more so for most ancient cities around the world. For this reason, archaeological evidence for a universal flood is largely lacking.

The best evidence for understanding the extent of the flood is the narrative of Genesis itself, although even here, the language of Scripture is open to interpretation. In normal speech, a word or phrase can be used both literally and as an idiom, and the same is true in the Bible. For example:

✠ The word *all*, which indicates how many mountains on earth were covered by the floodwaters (Gen. 7:19) as well as the number of people whom God promised to never destroy by flood again (Gen. 9:11), is used idiomatically to refer to only a limited portion of the earth in Genesis 41:57 and Deuteronomy 2:25.

✠ The word *covered* can mean "drenched with," as is its sense in Malachi 2:13, as well as "submerged by."

✠ The word for *earth* that is used repeatedly in the flood story is not *tevel* ("globe") but *eretz*, a word that can mean "earth" but typically just means "land," indicating something within the known horizon of those witnessing an event.

✠ On the other hand, the Hebrew term for the flood, *mabbul*, is something quite special, a word used only here in Genesis and in Psalm 29:10. We get our English word *cataclysm* from the corresponding Greek term, *kataklysmos*, an indication that the flood was indeed cataclysmic for everyone involved, regardless of its actual extent.

To summarize, it seems as though the arguments advanced for either a universal flood or a local flood based on archaeology, geology, or the text of Genesis are not watertight.

# MOUNTAINS OF ARARAT (Gen. 8:1–5 )

The water receded steadily from the earth. At the end of the hundred and fifty days the water had gone down, and on the seventeenth day of the seventh month the ark came to rest on the mountains of Ararat.

GENESIS 8:3–4

The flood stopped, and as the waters began to recede the ark rested on the mountains of Ararat. The plural term "mountains" indicates that the ark rested somewhere on the massive, rugged Ararat range which dominates the region of Lake Van in the eastern, Armenian portion of Turkey. The highest peak is Mount Ararat, 16,854 feet (5,137 m) in elevation. Expeditions to find remains of the ark began as early as medieval times and have become fairly frequent in recent decades, ever since pilots reported seeing the shape of an ark in the area during World War II. These have resulted in many claims about finding the ark, most of which are not properly verified and all of which are somewhat sensational. None of the alleged sightings have gained much acceptance.

Noah's exiting the ark (medieval mosaic in Palatine Chapel, Sicily)

# CHRONOLOGY OF THE FLOOD

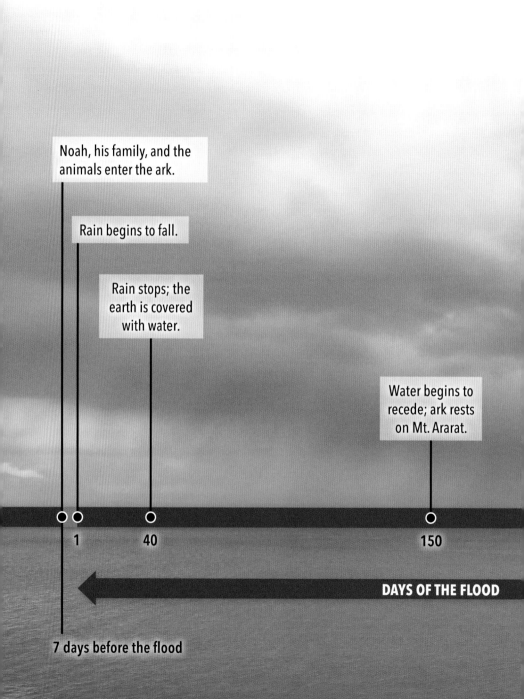

Noah, his family, and the animals enter the ark.

Rain begins to fall.

Rain stops; the earth is covered with water.

Water begins to recede; ark rests on Mt. Ararat.

1    40    150

DAYS OF THE FLOOD

7 days before the flood

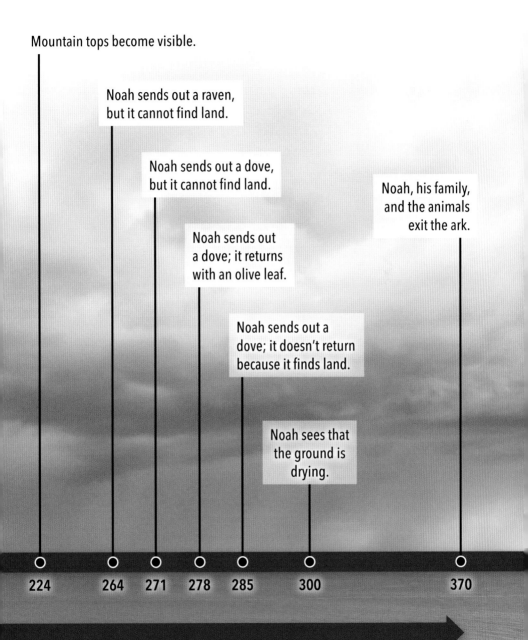

Mountain tops become visible.

Noah sends out a raven, but it cannot find land.

Noah sends out a dove, but it cannot find land.

Noah, his family, and the animals exit the ark.

Noah sends out a dove; it returns with an olive leaf.

Noah sends out a dove; it doesn't return because it finds land.

Noah sees that the ground is drying.

224     264    271    278    285        300                            370

## THE DOVE (Gen. 8:6–19)

When the dove returned to him in the evening, there in its beak was a freshly plucked olive leaf! Then Noah knew that the water had receded from the earth.

GENESIS 8:11

Noah sent a raven from the ark, then a dove three times to see if they could find dry land. On the dove's second trip, it plucked a fresh olive leaf. The olive tree, an evergreen, is an exceptionally hardy plant that can survive harsh conditions found throughout the Middle East—though probably not being totally inundated for an entire year. In the Bible, the olive tree, its leaves, and oil are indications of God's favor, blessing, life, and peace (see for example, Deut. 7:13; Ps. 128:3; Jer. 31:12). Noah, his family, and the animals left the ark after the earth was completely dry.

## THE RAINBOW (Gen. 8:20–9:17)

I establish my covenant with you: Never again will all life be destroyed by the waters of a flood; never again will there be a flood to destroy the earth.

GENESIS 9:11

Noah built an altar to the Lord and sacrificed animals on it. God made a covenant with Noah that he would never again destroy all humanity by a flood, sealing it with the sign of a rainbow. Genesis 9:8 contains the first use of the word *covenant* (Hebrew: *berit*) in the Bible. Although the details of the various covenants in the Old Testament differ, all carry the intent of restoring fellowship with people and bringing people back to God. This was an everlasting covenant made with Noah on behalf of all humanity.

## THE VINEYARD (Gen. 9:18–29)

The sons of Noah who came out of the ark were Shem, Ham and Japheth…. Noah, a man of the soil, proceeded to plant a vineyard. When he drank some of its wine, he became drunk and lay uncovered inside his tent.

GENESIS 9:18, 20

Noah planted a vineyard, got drunk, and responded by cursing and blessing his sons. This final episode in the Noah story shows that human sinfulness continued beyond the flood in spite of the judgments and blessings of God. This account sets the tone, and need, for the ongoing revelation of redemption that unfolds in the rest of the Bible.

While the story of Ham and Noah's nakedness has received a great deal of attention—most of it focused on a variety of sordid behaviors—there is nothing in the biblical story to suggest anything specific about the motives of either Noah or his sons. Nor can we conclude that Noah's curse of Ham's son Canaan, whatever its ramifications were at the time, is for all time in light of God's promise that all the peoples of the earth would be blessed through Abraham (Gen. 12:3).

Vineyard in valley near Mount Ararat, Armenia

# ANCIENT FLOOD STORIES

There are nearly three hundred ancient flood stories from across the globe. Most come from the Pacific Islands, Australia, the Americas, and some parts of Asia, with a few from Africa and Europe. It is possible to emphasize similarities between them and conclude that they point to a universal flood. It is also possible to conclude that they cannot point to a single event because they differ widely in many significant details and, in any case, devastating local floods that were remembered are a common occurrence.

Flood tablet of the Gilgamesh Epic

More significantly, the story of a flood sent by the gods to destroy humanity is found in several ancient Near Eastern myths.

✠ A Sumerian story tells of Zuisudra, a pious king who overhears a plan of the gods to destroy humankind by a flood. He saves himself in a boat and offers a sacrifice to the gods after the flood.

✠ The Old Babylonian Atra-hasis Epic relates how the gods send a seven-day flood to silence people on an over-crowded earth from making noise that bothered them. The protagonist Atra-hasis is saved by building a boat and taking some animals with him.

✠ Tablet 11 of the lengthy Gilgamesh Epic includes a flood story relating how Utnapishtim escaped a seven-day flood sent by the gods by taking "all living things" onto a boat with him. He used birds to check if the water had receded and offered a sacrifice upon disembarking.

These accounts come from the same general area as Noah and seem to point to the memory of a single, catastrophic event. They also indicate that the religious worldview with its many gods, out of which the Lord drew Noah and Abraham, differed widely from the revelation of God recorded in Genesis. For the pagan world, the flood was an event caused by capricious deities intent on protecting their own comfort. In Genesis, it is an act of moral judgment followed by grace with the intent of restoring wholeness, fellowship, and peace on earth and with God.

# NOAH'S THREE SONS AND THEIR SONS

**NOAH**

| JAPHETH | | HAM | SHEM |
|---------|---------|---------|---------|

| | | | |
|---------|---------|---------|---------|
| Gomer | Magog | Cush | Elam |
| Madai | Javan | Egypt (Mizraim) | Ashur |
| Tubal | Meshek | Put | Arphaxad |
| Tiras | | Canaan | Lud |
| | | | Aram |

# FIVE THEMES IN THE STORY OF NOAH'S ARK

## 1. God is sovereign and has the right to govern creation in any way that he sees fit.

We see this theme in two ways.

First, even though the story of the flood tells us many things that Noah did, it is not a story about him but about God. We can decipher things about Noah's character from his actions ("Noah did everything just as God commanded him;" Gen. 6:22; 7:5; 9:16) and from what the narrator tells us about him (Noah was "righteous, blameless and walked with

 God;" Gen. 6:9; 7:1), but Noah himself never says anything in the flood story. (Only after the flood, when Noah blesses and curses his sons, do we first hear him speak.) We do not get to hear his own voice about the wickedness of his day, about being told to build a massive ark, about his inmost hopes and fears, or even about his own motives and attitudes. It is only much later in the New Testament that the writer of Hebrews gives us a clue: Noah acted "in holy fear"

(Heb. 11:7). For this reason, we might consider Noah a silent character in the story, one who acts but is neither the one we get to hear nor the one driving the narrative. The one who does speak is God, to the extent of even providing the blueprints for the ark (Gen. 6:14–16). Throughout, it is God's words that hold power, express revelation, and define who Noah is and what Noah will be.

Second, the flood is depicted as a reversal of creation. In Genesis 1, the chaotic waters of the cosmic deep separate so dry land appears, a place described as "good," that is, suitable for human habitation (Gen. 1:9–10). With the flood, the mass of waters again overcome the earth, taking the possibility of human and animal life with them. The God who chooses to create can also choose to de-create if he so wishes (2 Peter 3:5–6).

## 2. Humans fail in their responsibility to live in righteous, helpful ways before God and others.

The ability to choose right from wrong is a part of what it means to be human—as is the tendency to often choose what is wrong. The story of Noah is a recognition of human depravity, a reality found at the very beginning of human history, reinforced throughout the biblical record, and shown to be equally obvious yet today. Just a few generations from creation, the earth and all people were already "corrupt … and full of violence" (Gen. 6:11). These are words that reveal the advancement of sin in all contexts: personal and social, as well as of the body, mind, and spirit.

## 3. Judgment is certain.

Judgment of human sin is real, and this act of judgment reveals a significant part of the character of God (Gen. 6:13; 7:4). Indeed, the judgment of the flood foreshadows an even greater judgment by God at the end of time (2 Peter 3:7).

> As it was in the days of Noah, so it will be at the coming of the Son of Man. For in the days before the flood, people were eating and drinking, marrying and giving in marriage, up to the day Noah entered the ark; and they knew nothing about what would happen until the flood came and took them all away. That is how it will be at the coming of the Son of Man.
>
> MATTHEW 24:37–39

## 4. We need to wait for God to act.

Noah and his family repeatedly waited for God to act:

- ✠ They waited for the rain to start after the door of the ark was closed (Gen. 7:10).

- ✠ They waited for the waters to subside after the rain had stopped (Gen. 8:1–5).

- ✠ They waited as the raven and dove were sent to see if the land could support life (Gen. 8:6, 12).

✠ They waited for God's command to leave of the ark (Gen. 8:13–19).

God knows the right time to act, as well as the extent to which he must act. The picture of a faithful remnant waiting for God—One who often seems to be waiting behind the scenes to act (1 Peter 3:20)—sets the tone for later stories in the Bible about God's people waiting for deliverance:

✠ The Hebrews under the bondage of Pharaoh in Egypt (Ex. 3:7–10).

✠ The remnant of Israel in exile in Babylon (Lam. 3:26).

✠ The psalmist seeking a silent God (Ps. 37:34; 38:15; 40:1).

✠ Believers waiting for the return of the Son of Man (Matt. 24:36–44).

## 5. The hope of salvation is certain, and with it the ability to start over.

The theme of salvation through the grace of God can be found throughout the narrative of Noah. The writer of Genesis says that the Lord was "grieved" that he had made mankind (Gen. 6:6), but also that Lamech had named his son Noah because he would bring "comfort" to a toilsome world (Gen. 5:28–29). Both verbs come from the same Hebrew root which means "moved to pity" (the name Noah may also come from the same word). So the story begins with hope found in God's choice of Noah, someone who would be delivered because of his righteousness and obedience (Gen. 6:9, 22; 7:1, 5, 9, 16).

First Peter 3:20–21 compares the flood to the waters of baptism, which also signal a coming up into new life. In Noah's story, this new life is pictured as a second creation, one that sets the world back to the way it was supposed to be.

✠ God pushed the waters away by a *ruah,* translated "spirit" in Genesis 1:2 and "wind" in Genesis 8:1.

✠ The birds and animals that exited the ark are described according to "kind," a term that echoes the categories at creation (Gen. 1:20–25; 8:17, 19). In both narratives—creation and Noah's ark—the birds and animals are commissioned to be "fruitful and increase in number" (Gen. 1:22; 8:17).

✠ People are still made in the image of God, with the mandate to be fruitful, multiply, and increase upon the earth (Gen. 1:27–28; 9:6–7).

✠ God planted a garden (Gen. 2:8) and Noah planted a vineyard (Gen. 9:20). Both were places of life and blessing, and both became the location of sin. While the specifics of Noah's drunken slumber are elusive, the reality of mankind's fall in Genesis 3 and the fact that personal choices have consequences is abundantly clear.

# CHAPTER 5

# Life of Abraham

magine being a close friend of an important person: the president of the country, an award-winning musician, the most popular sports star in town. It would increase your own reputation. Now imagine the God of infinite power choosing a mere mortal and calling him *friend.* Such a person existed. God called Abraham "my friend" (Isa. 41:8), and the apostle Paul said that Abraham was "the father of us all" (Rom. 4:16). Those are some impressive credentials!

The Bible does not tell us why God chose Abraham. However, we know that the call of Abraham marks a decisive point in the history of humanity in relation to God. From all the peoples of the earth, God chose a particular man, and from this man and his wife, God would begin a history that led directly to the birth, life, ministry, death, and resurrection of the Lord Jesus. But it all began with one man in an ancient city.

## MOVE FROM UR

A man and his family came out of the safety of their homeland. Terah, Abraham's father, left "Ur of the Chaldeans to go to Canaan" (Gen. 11:31). Genesis does not explain why Terah left the city of Ur, though it is possible that he was a traveling merchant or a seminomadic shepherd who followed trade roads looking for grazing land for his sheep. Either possibility could help explain why Terah was going to Canaan but instead settled in Harran. Not much is known about Terah. He was the father of at least three sons: Abraham (first named Abram), Nahor, and Haran. Terah likely practiced paganism, the religion of Ur. We do know that his was a family touched by tragedy in the form of death and infertility.

- ✠ Haran died while his father Terah was still alive, leaving Haran's son Lot and daughters Milkah and Iscah in the care of their grandfather (Gen. 11:28).

- ✠ Abraham married Sarah (Sarai), but the couple was childless "because [Sarai] was not able to conceive" (Gen. 11:30).

# A DECISIVE CALL

The Lord told Abraham to go to a land away from his home. How did Abraham know the Lord? How did God reveal himself to Abraham? Was it a vision, a dream, or a voice? As readers, we can understand that God was doing something extraordinary, but we do not know whether Abraham understood it the same way or even why he obeyed this call. We do know that he listened to God and traveled as he was told. Much later, the writer of the letter to the Hebrews explained that Abraham obeyed "by faith" (Heb. 11:9). It was his faithful answer to God's call that marks the beginning of a new history—the history of salvation. Faith means trusting in God—in who God is, in what he is willing and able to do, and in humbly trusting that his guidance will lead to abundant life.

> The Lord had said to Abram, "Go from your country, your people and your father's household to the land I will show you."
>
> GENESIS 12:1

## THE FAMILY TREE OF TERAH

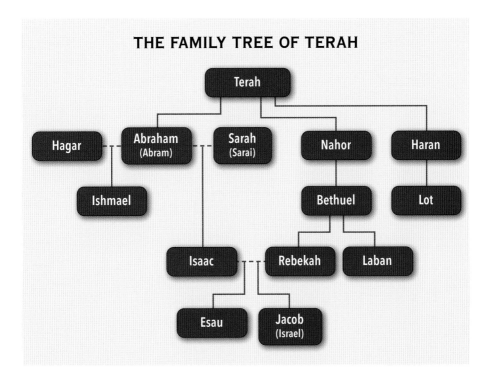

# A KING'S COVENANT AND FRIENDSHIP

Abraham's journey of faith was filled with grief and joy, doubts and triumphs, and dangers and victories. In this journey, we see how God related to Abraham in two ways: a formal relationship as king through a covenant and an intimate relationship as a friend.

From the first chapter of Genesis, kingship is the main metaphor used in the Bible to describe God's activities and relationships. God is King. In the ancient world, kings related to others in the kingdom primarily through covenants. There were two main types of covenants between a king and his subjects: conditional and unconditional.

✠ In a *conditional* covenant, the king claimed complete authority over his subjects, and the king pledged to offer protection and provision on condition of the loyalty of the subjects. In other words, the subjects pledged loyalty and service to the king and expected in return the king's protection and favor.

✠ In an *unconditional* covenant, the king pledged a royal favor on behalf of a subject, perhaps to reward a special service to the king. The favor could take different forms. One common form was a royal grant of land.

| COVENANT TYPE | SCRIPTURE | DESCRIPTION |
| --- | --- | --- |
| Unconditional | Gen. 15:9–21 | God promised to give Abraham's descendants the land. The covenant was sealed with an animal sacrifice rite. |
| Conditional | Gen. 17:1–27 | God confirmed his covenant with Abraham (Gen. 17:2) and made a commitment to Abraham ("As for me…" Gen. 17:4). He then specified Abraham's commitment ("As for you…" Gen. 17:9). God reaffirmed his promise of land, and Abraham agreed to keep the sign of the covenant: circumcision. |

## JESUS, OUR FRIEND FOR THE JOURNEY

Just as Abraham was God's friend, believers are Jesus's friends (John 15:14). Jesus has not stopped being the King of kings, and when he returns, "every knee should bow, in heaven and on earth and underneath the earth, and every tongue acknowledge that Jesus Christ is Lord" (Phil. 2:10–11). He wants to be our companion on our journey, the one whom we can trust, whom we can confide in with our deepest secrets and fears, whom we can rely on when the journey is too difficult, and with whom we can share our joys in thanksgiving and praise.

Even before Abraham, God had shown that he wanted to relate to humanity in an intimate way: in the garden of Eden, God had acted as a careful, loving gardener when he created humanity, and he had strolled in the cool of the evening with his creation.

Abraham's story illustrates a journey of friendship; it shows that God is reliable, full of grace, forgiving, and worthy of trust, praise, and glory. It shows us that deciding to accompany God on this journey of faith is the wisest decision a person can make—the decision that leads to life, blessing, and the promised land.

> But you, Israel, my servant, Jacob, whom I have chosen, you descendants of Abraham my friend.
>
> ISAIAH 41:8

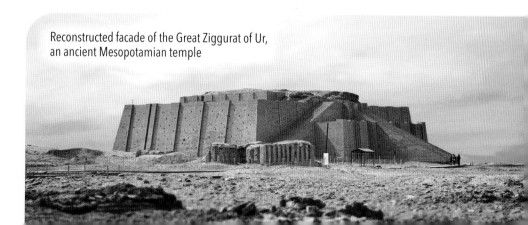

Reconstructed facade of the Great Ziggurat of Ur, an ancient Mesopotamian temple

# THE BLESSING

God created a good world and blessed it. But life may not always seem to be a blessing; much goes wrong, as we see it did in the first chapters of Genesis. Yet the road toward restoration begins with blessing.

Blessings are not rewards for good behavior or correct beliefs. Blessings are deeply tied to God's creative activity. When God created the universe, he created life because he is a God of life, a God of the living. His actions are life giving. Blessings, then, are favors through which God gives life—abundant life—to his creation.

God blessed Abraham. This moment occurred at the beginning of a long road that would end with the coming of the Messiah.

> I will make you into a great nation, and I will bless you; I will make your name great, and you will be a blessing.
>
> GENESIS 12:2

In the case of Abraham, God's blessings would occur in two main ways: descendants and land. Children and land were essential components of people's identities during ancient times, and both are connected with Genesis 3. In the garden of Eden, God's punishments were related to bearing children (childbirth would be painful; Gen. 3:16) and land (man would have to work the ground to produce food; Gen. 3:17–19). God's promise to bless Abraham with descendants and land were meant to counteract the effects of the curse. These blessings that would begin with Abraham's family would eventually extend to all the nations of the world (Gen. 12:3; Gal. 3:14). The blessings were just the beginning of God's plans.

| DESCENDANTS | LAND |
| --- | --- |
| God promised to give Abraham descendants as numerous as the dust of the earth and the stars in the sky (Gen. 13:16; 15:5). With Abraham and Sarah, God began a new history of blessing and salvation. | God promised to give the land of Canaan to Abraham's descendants, a place where they would live and fulfill their calling as God's people (Gen. 12:6-7; 13:14-17; 15:7, 18; 17:8). |

# A JOURNEY OF FAITH

Abraham's journey was one of faith. He traveled away from his family and the city in which he had made his home and into a future that remained unknown. He was not a young man—he was seventy-five years old (Gen. 12:4)—and, surely, he had had a full life in his city. But along with his wife Sarah, his nephew Lot, and all of his possessions, including his servants, Abraham traveled from Harran to Canaan—a trip of over 400 miles (650 km). There, "the LORD appeared to Abram" (Gen. 12:7).

This simple statement about God's appearance carries a great deal of meaning. In that part of the world at that time, the people of each city believed that a particular god or goddess protected their city, and each city had a temple where the people believed their god or goddess lived and was their place of worship. These deities normally did not travel from city to city. But the God who had talked to Abraham in Harran appeared to him in Canaan. The Lord did not simply send Abraham on a journey like some fabled hero who had to defeat obstacles using his skills and abilities. Rather, God traveled with him. In this story, Abraham is not the hero; God is the hero.

## NAME CHANGES

God changed the names of Abram and Sarai to Abraham and Sarah (Gen. 17:5, 15).

- ✠ *Abram* most likely means "exalted father," and it probably was a reference to Abraham's pagan past. *Abraham* means "father of many," signaling God's promise to give Abraham and Sarah offspring as abundant as the stars in the heavens.

- ✠ *Sarai* means "my princess," though the name was probably longer and included the name of a goddess. *Sarah* means "princess," and it stands on its own, probably signaling the fact that God had given her back her dignity, her value as a person.

The name changes are another signal of the beginning of the new history—the history of restoration.

But this journey was not a walk in the park.

> Now there was a famine in the land, and Abram went
> down to Egypt to live there for a while because the
> famine was severe.
>
> GENESIS 12:10

In Abraham's world, people believed that the gods of rain, land, and fertility caused famines. Famine was a consequence of human rebellion, a part of the original curse. Abraham's detour to Egypt reminds us immediately that, although God had begun the process of restoration, the curse still affected the fertility of the ground and people's lives.

Through this episode in Abraham's life, as others that happened later, we see him as a person we can relate to, a person with doubts, one who had failings and made mistakes, but one whom God loved, blessed, guided, and protected.

## God Meets Abraham's Fears and Doubts

Though Abraham was a man who trusted God, at times, he also had fears and doubts. His fear led him to lie to Pharaoh and King Abimelek about his wife in order to ensure his own safety and profit. Although Abraham was a great host, he was not a very good guest with Pharaoh and Abimelek. He deceived Pharaoh in Egypt and then Abimelek in Gerar (Gen. 12:10–20; 20:1–18).

Pharaoh Nebhepetre Mentuhotep II, one of the pharaohs who ruled
during the era of the patriarchs in the Bible

| ABRAHAM'S FEAR OR DOUBT | GOD'S FAITHFUL ACTION |
|---|---|
| Abraham feared Pharaoh, so he lied about the identity of his wife (Gen. 12:10–20). | "The LORD inflicted serious diseases on Pharaoh and his household because of Abram's wife Sarai" (Gen. 12:17). |
| Abraham doubted God's power to give him and Sarah a son (Gen. 17:15–19). | "Now the LORD was gracious to Sarah as he had said, and the LORD did for Sarah what he had promised. Sarah became pregnant and bore a son to Abraham in his old age, at the very time God had promised him" (Gen. 21:1–2). |
| Abraham feared King Abimelek, so again, he lied about the identity of his wife (Gen. 20:1–18). | "God came to Abimelek in a dream one night and said to him, 'You are as good as dead because of the woman you have taken; she is a married woman'" (Gen. 20:3). |

## Man's Schemes and God's Miracles

Despite what common sense suggested, Abraham showed his trust in God that God's promise of a son would become a reality. But Sarah did not trust, and in time, Abraham also began to doubt. At his wife's insistence, Abraham had a child with Sarah's Egyptian slave Hagar. Although Hagar's child Ishmael was Abraham's son, God made it clear that Ishmael was not the promised son.

God had not visited Sarah, nor had she witnessed God making a covenant with her husband, so when God visited Abraham in his camp, Sarah, not knowing that the visitor was God, laughed that the promise would or could be fulfilled, given her advanced age (Gen. 18:12). But God's promise came to pass, and Isaac was born to Abraham and Sarah (Gen. 21:1–7).

# ABRAHAM'S JOURNEY TO CANAAN

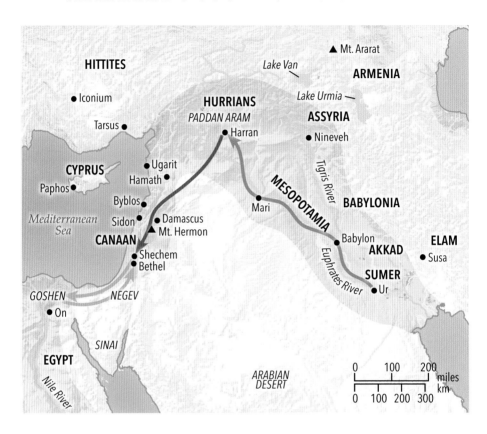

> ──────▶ Ur to Harran Gen. 11:31
>
> ━━━━━▶ Harran to Canaan Gen. 12:1-8
>
> ┈┈┈┈┈▶ To Egypt and Return to Canaan Gen. 12:9-10; 13:1-4

## THE TESTS

Abraham's character was tested on his journey of faith. He was a hospitable person. Hospitality in the world of seminomadic peoples was vital for survival. Hospitality allowed for weary travelers to renew their strength in peace and safety. Traditionally, the host would provide food, a place to rest, and water for the guests to clean up and refresh themselves. Abraham proved to be a loving and welcoming host with Lot and his family and with God and his messengers while they were on their way to Sodom.

Another test of Abraham's character was his relationships with other people. He was a peace-loving and loyal person, and his love and commitment toward his nephew Lot are remarkable illustrations of this. When conflict arose between Abraham and Lot's shepherds, Abraham voluntarily separated from Lot and agreed to take the less appealing land to keep peace with him and his household.

> So Abram said to Lot, "Let's not have any quarreling between you and me, or between your herders and mine, for we are close relatives."
>
> GENESIS 13:8

Abraham also risked his life and rescued Lot when a coalition of kings captured Lot and his possessions. Finally, Abraham interceded with God to spare Lot and his family from the imminent judgment against Sodom and Gomorrah where Lot lived.

Hebron mountains

Abraham's trust in God was also tested when God told him to offer his only son as a sacrifice.

> Then God said, "Take your son, your only son, whom you love—Isaac—and go to the region of Moriah. Sacrifice him there as a burnt offering on a mountain I will show you."
>
> GENESIS 22:2

On Mount Moriah, Abraham was ready to do as God had instructed—an unimaginable act of trust and faith. God stopped Abraham, however, as

Nuzi tablet with cuneiform writing, one of the earliest types of writing which developed in Mesopotamia

he raised his knife to kill Isaac, who lay tied on a stone altar. Instead, God provided a ram for the sacrifice, sparing Isaac.

Pushing the limits of human trust in God, Abraham showed that he had come to trust in God completely, and God also showed that he is a God worthy of trust. God's promise to Abraham would indeed be fulfilled—through Isaac, Abraham's only son. What God promises will come to pass.

Abraham's faith continued to grow, even as he came to the end of his life. When Sarah died, he bought a field in the land of Canaan, the land that God had promised to Abraham's descendants.

> I am a foreigner and stranger among you. Sell me some property for a burial site here so I can bury my dead.
>
> GENESIS 23:4

That symbolic action anticipated the day when God would give the land to Abraham's descendants, the children of Israel. And when Abraham eventually died, he too was buried in Canaan, beside Sarah in the cave near Mamre in Hebron (Gen. 25:9–10).

# ABRAHAM'S JOURNEYS IN CANAAN

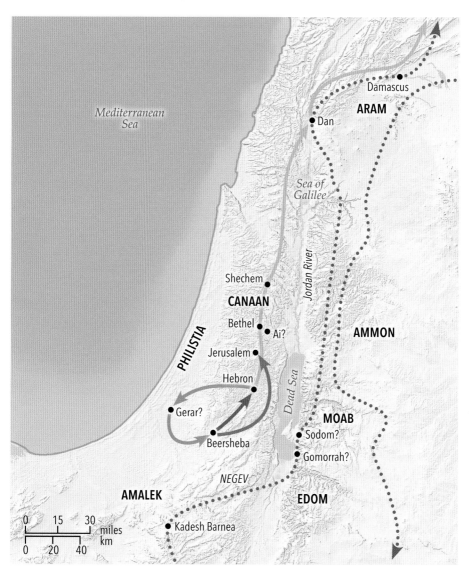

······▶ Campaigns of the northern kings against the Canaanite kings. Gen. 14:1–12

▶ Abraham rescues Lot from the northern kings. Gen. 13:18; 14:13–16

▶ Abraham lives in Gerar and Beersheba. Gen. 20:1; 21:31–34

▶ God tests Abraham in Moriah near Jerusalem. Gen. 22:1–19

▶ Abraham and Sarah are buried in Hebron. Gen. 23:19; 25:7–10

# LIFE OF ABRAHAM TIME LINE

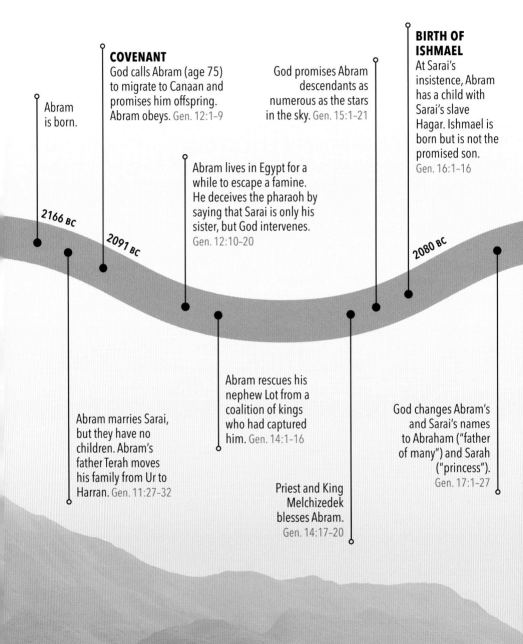

Abram is born.

2166 BC

**COVENANT**
God calls Abram (age 75) to migrate to Canaan and promises him offspring. Abram obeys. Gen. 12:1–9

2091 BC

Abram lives in Egypt for a while to escape a famine. He deceives the pharaoh by saying that Sarai is only his sister, but God intervenes. Gen. 12:10–20

God promises Abram descendants as numerous as the stars in the sky. Gen. 15:1–21

**BIRTH OF ISHMAEL**
At Sarai's insistence, Abram has a child with Sarai's slave Hagar. Ishmael is born but is not the promised son. Gen. 16:1–16

2080 BC

Abram marries Sarai, but they have no children. Abram's father Terah moves his family from Ur to Harran. Gen. 11:27-32

Abram rescues his nephew Lot from a coalition of kings who had captured him. Gen. 14:1–16

Priest and King Melchizedek blesses Abram. Gen. 14:17–20

God changes Abram's and Sarai's names to Abraham ("father of many") and Sarah ("princess"). Gen. 17:1–27

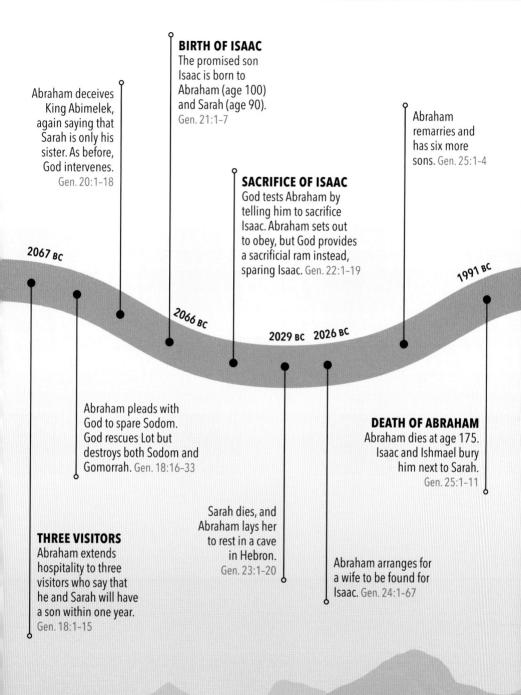

**BIRTH OF ISAAC**
The promised son
Isaac is born to
Abraham (age 100)
and Sarah (age 90).
Gen. 21:1–7

Abraham deceives
King Abimelek,
again saying that
Sarah is only his
sister. As before,
God intervenes.
Gen. 20:1–18

Abraham
remarries and
has six more
sons. Gen. 25:1–4

**SACRIFICE OF ISAAC**
God tests Abraham by
telling him to sacrifice
Isaac. Abraham sets out
to obey, but God provides
a sacrificial ram instead,
sparing Isaac. Gen. 22:1–19

2067 BC

1991 BC

2066 BC

2029 BC   2026 BC

Abraham pleads with
God to spare Sodom.
God rescues Lot but
destroys both Sodom and
Gomorrah. Gen. 18:16–33

**DEATH OF ABRAHAM**
Abraham dies at age 175.
Isaac and Ishmael bury
him next to Sarah.
Gen. 25:1–11

Sarah dies, and
Abraham lays her
to rest in a cave
in Hebron.
Gen. 23:1–20

**THREE VISITORS**
Abraham extends
hospitality to three
visitors who say that
he and Sarah will have
a son within one year.
Gen. 18:1–15

Abraham arranges for
a wife to be found for
Isaac. Gen. 24:1–67

Dates are approximate.

# CHAPTER 6

# Life of Joseph

T he story of Joseph teaches about faith and trust, and God's power in times of suffering. It is also a thrilling story of a seventeen-year-old boy who was …

✠ favored by his father;

✠ resented by his ten older brothers;

✠ thrown into a pit in the wilderness; and

✠ sold into slavery and never returned home.

Later, just when it appeared his life was improving, Joseph was…

✠ stalked by someone powerful and vengeful;

✠ falsely accused and imprisoned;

✠ abandoned in jail without friends or supporters to defend him; and

✠ forgotten by people who owed him a favor.

But throughout the misery, God was there with Joseph. His story gives hope on four levels.

| 1 | Personal | God has a purpose in suffering. God grew Joseph from immaturity to strength and mercy. |
|---|----------|---------------------------------------------------------------------------------------|
| 2 | Family | God used bad circumstances to save Joseph's family and change their hearts. |
| 3 | Nationally | God used Joseph's misfortunes to save many lives, and to set up the rest of the biblical story that leads to the saving of the world through Christ. |
| 4 | Beyond | God used the events in Joseph's story to bring blessing to the world long past biblical days. Believers today are part of God's larger plan that calls for patience and trust during times of suffering. Just as God blessed Joseph's faithfulness, God will bless faithfulness today. |

# BEGINNING OF THE PROMISE

This story begins long before Joseph's birth. It begins with his great-grandfather Abraham, a nomadic sheep and goat herder who lived in the dry, hot region of the Middle East known as Canaan. Although Joseph can be considered the main character in Genesis 37–50, the story is really about God and his promise to Abraham's descendants, including Joseph.

God had appeared to Abraham and made two promises: "I will make you a great nation … and all the peoples on earth will be blessed through you" (Gen. 12:1–2).

God's promise to Abraham changed the direction of humanity. Human disobedience and rebellion turned God's creation upside down. Instead of being a good and blessed creation, human rebellion resulted in a cursed creation and a cursed history (see Gen. 1–3). God promised Abraham to start a new history of blessing with him and his family. This family was certainly not an ideal family; it resembled many families today, with struggles, deep problems, sadness, and grief.

## A Dysfunctional Family

The narrative begins with Joseph's father Jacob living "in the land of Canaan" (Gen. 37:1). This simple statement is a reminder in the story that God is implementing his promise to Abraham. The biblical narrative then introduces Joseph and his brothers. It is immediately clear that their relationships are broken and that the potential for conflict is great.

> Joseph, a young man of seventeen, was tending the flocks with his brothers, the sons of Bilhah and the sons of Zilpah, his father's wives, and he brought their father a bad report about them.
>
> GENESIS 37:2

## Playing Favorites

Joseph was Jacob's youngest and favorite son. This favoritism is evident in two clues in a few short lines in the story.

1.  The "coat of many colors" (or "richly ornamented robe") was a gift from Jacob to Joseph (Gen. 37:3). Whatever exactly the robe was, it was a special and precious garment indicating that Joseph was not meant for a life of fieldwork like Jacob's other sons. The Bible describes a similar robe in only one other place, 2 Samuel 13:18. There, King David's daughter Tamar wears a robe described as "the kind of garment the virgin daughters of the king wore."

2.  The other telling comment about Jacob's favoritism is of "a bad report" Joseph brings about his brothers (Gen. 37:2). Jacob foolishly sent the favored son to check on his older brothers. By this time, Joseph's actions and attitudes have hurt his relationship and angered his brothers. The expression "bad report" is also found in Psalm 31:13, Jeremiah 20:10, and Ezekiel 36:3 where it is used for the whispering of hostile people.

## THE WAGES OF DECEIT

Jacob's relationship with his sons reflects a lifetime of deceit. Jacob deceived his father Isaac for his blessing—cheating his brother Esau out of that blessing. Jacob fled his brother's anger and traveled to Harran to live with his uncle Laban. There, Jacob fell in love with Laban's youngest daughter Rachel. However, Laban made Jacob work seven years for his daughter, but then he gave his oldest daughter Leah to Jacob in marriage instead. Jacob had to work another seven years for Rachel.

Jacob's love for Rachel was always greater than his love for Leah. However, God granted Leah many sons from Jacob, whereas Rachel was not able to give birth. Rachel finally bore a son to Jacob: Joseph. Jacob's love for Joseph became an extension of his love for Rachel.

## Joseph's Dream

Joseph's older brothers resent their father's favoritism as much as Joseph's attitude. Young Joseph fails to understand the depth of his brothers' loathing toward him. With little tact and wisdom, Joseph shares his dreams with his family. One night, Joseph dreams that his brothers and parents bow before him. The Bible does not say that Joseph's dreams were from God. In fact, we do not know that is the case until the end of the story when the dreams become reality. For Joseph's brothers, these dreams also become the straw that breaks the camel's back.

## Deceiving the Deceiver

The strained relationships among family members anticipate a potentially tragic ending. Jacob sends Joseph to check on his brothers who were herding sheep far away—an unwise decision considering the previous "bad report" from Joseph and the already weak relationships among his children. Joseph's brothers find a perfect opportunity to be rid of their youngest brother. The brothers throw Joseph in a pit and want to kill him. Reuben hopes to rescue Joseph, but Judah, one of two eldest brothers, argues that it is better to make some money from the deal. Instead of killing Joseph, they sell him to a trading caravan going to Egypt. Joseph, although alive, ends up as a slave in Egypt. Jacob is cruelly deceived by his sons, who return with a bloodied robe and a terrible lie: Joseph is dead.

# JACOB'S JOURNEYS

Jacob, migrated to Harran, where he married Leah and Rachel, and had twelve sons. Jacob returned to Canaan and the Lord renamed him "Israel."

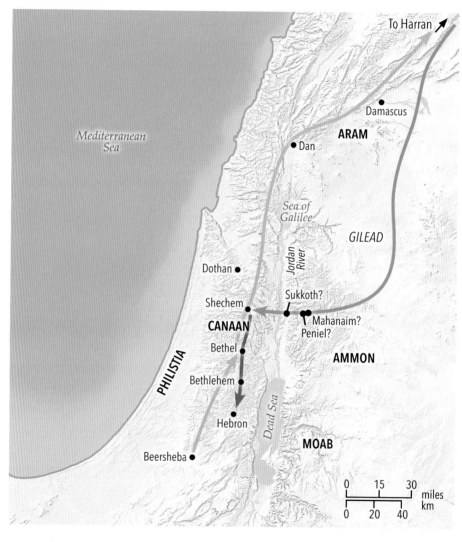

Beersheba to Harran Gen. 28:10–29:1

Harran to Shechem Gen. 31:21; 32:1–32; 33:17–20

Shechem to Hebron Gen. 35:1–29

# JOSEPH'S ROUTE TO EGYPT

Near Dothan, where Joseph's brothers were grazing their flocks, Joseph's jealous brothers sold him to Ishmaelite (Midianite) traders on their way to Egypt.

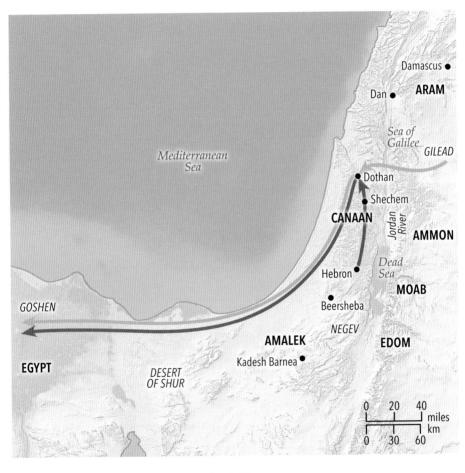

Damascus •

Dan •    **ARAM**

*Sea of Galilee*    *GILEAD*

*Mediterranean Sea*

• Dothan
• Shechem

**CANAAN**

*Jordan River*

**AMMON**

*Dead Sea*

Hebron •

• Beersheba

**MOAB**

*GOSHEN*

*NEGEV*

**EGYPT**

**AMALEK**    **EDOM**

Kadesh Barnea •

*DESERT OF SHUR*

| 0 | 20 | 40 |
| miles |

| 0 | 30 | 60 |
| km |

➤ Route of Joseph Gen. 37:12–17, 28

➤ Route of the Ishmaelite Traders Gen. 37:25–28

# A STORY WITHIN A STORY

Right in the middle of the story of Joseph, the book of Genesis pauses and tells a separate story (Gen. 38). Joseph's brother Judah, now a grown man with three sons, tries to deceive his daughter-in-law Tamar by promising to follow the marriage laws that will protect her but actually refusing to carry them out. As time goes by, Tamar realizes she has been denied her proper rights. She turns around and deceives Judah by disguising herself as a prostitute and bearing Judah's twin sons.

In a family with a history of lying and violence, betrayal, and hatred, how did God change Judah's heart? Judah had to admit that his actions had been wrong—far worse than his daughter-in-law's. He admitted that Tamar was more righteous than he was. Judah, a man unable to regret his mistreatment of his brother Joseph and his father, who lies and does injustice to his daughter-in-law, is a changed man. He is finally able to confess his error and make things right for Tamar. While Joseph is in Egypt, God starts the change in Joseph's brothers.

## JACOB'S FAMILY TREE

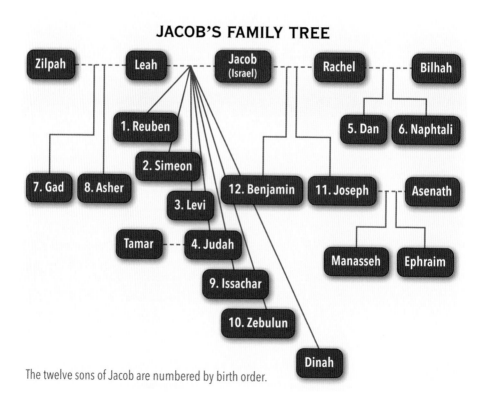

The twelve sons of Jacob are numbered by birth order.

## From Powerless to Potiphar's

Joseph goes from being the beloved son to being sold as a powerless slave in a powerful Egyptian officer's home. Potiphar is the captain of Pharaoh's bodyguard. In spite of this terrible reversal of fortunes, Scripture tells us, that "the Lord was with Joseph" (Gen. 39:2). We do not know if Joseph, the shepherd boy, knew the language. It is unlikely that he was educated at the level of the Egyptian upper class, but the Bible is clear that Joseph does not give up. He works hard and contributes to Potiphar's household. Every small responsibility he handles is successful. Over time, Potiphar realizes that the Lord is with this slave, and Potiphar puts Joseph in charge of everything he owns.

## Rejection and Revenge

Potiphar's wife wants Joseph to sleep with her, but Joseph refuses, calling her proposed actions:

- ✠ a breach of his responsibilities;

- ✠ a betrayal of Potiphar who has trusted him; and

- ✠ a sin against God.

> With me in charge, my master does not concern himself with anything in the house; everything he owns he has entrusted to my care. No one is greater in this house than I am. My master has withheld nothing from me except you, because you are his wife. How then could I do such a wicked thing and sin against God?
>
> GENESIS 39:8–9

Potiphar's wife will not take no for an answer, so she stalks him. Day after day she talks with him, trying to seduce him. But one day, they are in the house alone and she grabs his clothing. Her grip must have been strong, because to get away he had to shed that garment and run outside. This final rejection leads her to revenge. She calls out to the men in the household and claims she has been attacked. When Potiphar hears, he is angry and throws Joseph in jail.

# FROM POTIPHAR'S TO PRISON

Joseph is not given a trial. He is unfairly thrown into a jail for the king's prisoners. It was another reversal of fortunes. A good man treated wrongly, framed, betrayed by his employer's wife, despite his flawless work. No one would blame Joseph for becoming angry and bitter, but he did not. In fact, "the LORD was with Joseph" (Gen. 39:2). Joseph used his administrative skills to help, and over time was put in charge of all the prisoners and the prison organization. He found favor with the chief jailer, whose confidence in Joseph was so high that he did not even supervise Joseph.

Two new prisoners, a cupbearer and a baker from Pharaoh's household, were placed in the jail for offending their master. Joseph was put in charge of them and took care of them for a long time. One night both men had troubling dreams, and in the morning Joseph realized they were sad because there was no one to explain the dreams to them. (Notice how Joseph, who had been insensitive to his brothers' feelings, now cared about others.) Joseph offered to interpret the dreams and was intentional about giving credit to God rather than to himself, despite having a reputation as a clever man.

> "We both had dreams, … but there is no one to interpret them." Then Joseph said to them, "Do not interpretations belong to God? Tell me your dreams."
>
> GENESIS 40:8

| | DREAM | INTERPRETATION FROM GOD |
|---|---|---|
| Cupbearer | A vine with three branches producing grapes which were squeezed and the juice given to Pharaoh. | In three days, Pharaoh will give the cupbearer back his job. |
| Baker | Carrying three baskets of bread for Pharaoh on his head. Birds came and ate them. | In three days, Pharaoh will have the baker executed. |

After interpreting the dreams, Joseph asks the cupbearer to remember him, to help him get out of prison. Within three days, both predictions come true. The cupbearer is restored to his place of privilege and the baker is executed. But the cupbearer forgets about Joseph, and Joseph continues to live in a dungeon several more years.

## PHARAOH'S DREAMS

One night, Pharaoh has two dreams that none of his magicians and wise men can interpret. Suddenly, the cupbearer remembers Joseph and tells about the Hebrew slave who interpreted his own dream two years prior. Pharaoh calls for Joseph, who has to shave and change clothes from his prison garb to appear before Pharaoh.

Pharaoh says, "I have heard it said about you, that when you hear a dream you can interpret it."

Joseph replies, "It is not in me; God will give Pharaoh a favorable answer."

When Joseph hears the dreams, he calls them "one and the same" (Gen. 41:25). The dreams are parallel and have the same message.

| | DREAM | INTERPRETATION FROM GOD |
|---|---|---|
| 1 | Seven cows come out of the Nile River. They are sleek and fat and grazing. Seven more cows come out of the Nile. These are ugly and gaunt. They eat the sleek, fat cows. | After seven years of abundance in the land of Egypt, seven years of famine will ravage the land. The double dream means that God will surely do this and do it soon. |
| 2 | Seven ears of plump good grain appear on one single stalk. Then seven thin and scorched ears sprout up and swallow the plump ears. | |

With this interpretation, Joseph recommends that Pharaoh find a wise supervisor to put in charge, then appoint overseers who will collect and store one fifth of the annual food harvests in Egypt for the seven good years. This reserve will keep the people of Egypt from perishing during the seven years of famine.

Pharaoh sets Joseph over all of Egypt, gives him his signet ring of authority, clothes him in fine linen and emblems of power, and puts him in a chariot and makes him his second in command. For thirteen years, Joseph had been a slave in Egypt and now he is second in command and is given every honor of status and fame and a notable marriage to Asenath, the daughter of the priest of On. At age thirty, he is given the responsibility to travel through Egypt and supervise the storage of grain in locations owned by Pharaoh. He is so successful, and the abundance is so great, that even he can no longer keep track of the massive amounts of harvest.

## OF DREAMS AND GODS

Dreams were important in the ancient world, especially in Egypt. The Egyptians had texts that priests would use to interpret dreams. Dreams were windows into the world of the gods. For this reason, priests were the people who could best interpret them.

When Pharaoh asks Joseph to interpret his dreams, Joseph replies, "I cannot do it, but God will give Pharaoh the answer he desires" (Gen. 41:16). Joseph claims that his God can do something Pharaoh's gods have failed to do. Joseph is confident because, as he said before, "Do not interpretations belong to God?" (Gen. 40:8). It is an astonishing claim. Although the Egyptians were quite open to other people's gods, they were confident their own gods were superior. Joseph's claim suggests that the interpretation of dreams belongs to God because revelation through dreams comes from God. Joseph is proclaiming God's superiority over the Egyptians gods.

# JOSEPH'S BROTHERS IN EGYPT

When the famine hits, Joseph's brothers arrive in Egypt on a mission to save their family from starvation. This surprise encounter sparks a series of events that transforms Joseph and his brothers' lives forever.

His brothers arrive and bow down to the Egyptian lord.

> Although Joseph recognized his brothers, they did not recognize him.
>
> GENESIS 42:8

The statement reminds the readers of much earlier in the story when the brothers were asking their father to *recognize* Joseph's bloodied garment (the Hebrew word for "recognize" can also be translated as "examine;" Gen. 37:32). This recognition brings Joseph's memories back like a flood. As his son Manasseh's name implies, Joseph had been able to forget his difficult past (*manasseh* probably means "to forget;" Gen. 41:51). Now the memories, the pain, the anger, and the doubts arise with renewed impetus.

Joseph speaks harshly to his brothers and accuses them of being spies. This is not a light issue! The brothers understand immediately that they are in mortal peril. The Egyptian lord does not have to offer proof for his accusation and could execute them at any moment with a simple command. Sheer terror makes them tell the truth about themselves: "We are all the sons of one man. Your servants are honest men, not spies" (Gen. 42:11). Their claim is another way to say they have clan responsibilities.

Joseph tests their claim of being honest men and accuses them again of being spies. The brothers insist, "Your servants were twelve brothers, the sons of one man, who lives in the land of Canaan. The youngest is now with our father, and one is no more" (Gen. 42:13). Joseph learns more about his family: his father is still alive and his youngest brother Benjamin is with him.

In this brief episode, we can imagine a divided Joseph, a man full of anger and overwhelmed with memories but also full of wisdom and responsibility. Joseph is a changed man. However, if Joseph is changed, have his brothers changed at all? Are they still the same foolish men willing to destroy a person's life to quench their anger?

Joseph tests his brothers more than once, first by hiding his true identity, then by making them leave Simeon as a guarantee that they would return with their youngest brother. The brothers fail to persuade their father to let them bring Benjamin with them to Egypt. Jacob, a broken man, bitterly reminds them of Joseph. Jacob refuses to trust them with Benjamin's life for he fears the ending will be as tragic as that of Joseph's. Reuben makes a proposal: the lives of his two children for the life of Benjamin. Jacob has already lost two children, Joseph and Simeon, so why would he risk losing Benjamin and two grandchildren? Reuben's proposal is reckless. Jacob decides not to send Benjamin with them.

Because the famine is so severe, Jacob's sons have no choice but to return to Egypt for grain. Judah steps forward and makes a wise suggestion. If something happens to Benjamin, Judah accepts the guilt

and responsibility himself. It is a wise and mature proposal. In the ancient world, a verbal promise was not a thing lightly taken. Verbal commitments were a guarantee of action. Because of Judah's promise, Jacob reluctantly accepts. The brothers are on their way back to Egypt.

Joseph continues the charade. He knows his brothers will return for Simeon; but would they do the same for Benjamin?

Through yet another test, Joseph forces his brothers to demonstrate the kind of men they have become. When Benjamin is falsely found guilty of stealing a silver cup, Joseph quickly and angrily issues the punishment: Benjamin is to remain as his slave. But Judah steps up and demonstrates his moral quality and maturity. He explains to Joseph his own promise to Jacob. He says, "Now then, please, let your servant remain here as my lord's slave in place of the boy, and let the boy return with his brothers" (Gen. 44:33). Judah has changed; he is no longer the self-centered man who once chose personal gain over his brother's safety, and personal security over his daughter-in-law's righteous claim.

## RECONCILIATION

Joseph cannot control himself and reveals his identity. While Joseph is moved to tears, his brothers are terrified when they finally recognize him. Joseph makes this wise and powerful statement:

> But God sent me ahead of you to preserve for you
> a remnant on earth and to save your lives by a great
> deliverance. So then, it was not you who sent me here,
> but God.
>
> GENESIS 45:7–8

Joseph and Pharaoh invite Jacob and his family to live in Egypt. Before leaving Canaan, the land God had promised to Abraham, Jacob has a dream. In the dream, God tells him, "I am God, the God of your father...."

Do not be afraid to go down to Egypt, for I will make you into a great nation there. I will go down to Egypt with you, and I will surely bring you back again" (Gen. 46:3–4). God is renewing his promise to Abraham. God will make Abraham's descendants into a great nation in Egypt. Then, he will give this new nation a land where he will dwell with them.

Years later, when their father Jacob dies, Joseph's brothers still wonder if Joseph will take revenge against them. Instead, Joseph says:

> Don't be afraid. Am I in the place of God? You intended to harm me, but God intended it for good to accomplish what is now being done, the saving of many lives.
>
> GENESIS 50:19–20

# THE GOD WHO WAS THERE

Throughout the story of Joseph, we find God at crucial moments. He is not always acting directly, but his presence is constant, causing or enabling all possible movement: geographic, moral, from foolishness to wisdom. Through this movement in Joseph's story, God redeems a broken family.

## SUFFERING AND WISDOM

Although Joseph's story does not explain every case of suffering and grief, it instructs us on how to acquire the necessary wisdom that will allow us to face such experiences. The Bible recognizes that doctrinal statements are not enough to deal with suffering and grief. Wisdom allows us to see life from God's perspective. When we can see life through wisdom, we can trust that God will allow "neither death nor life, neither angels nor demons, neither the present nor the future, nor any powers, neither height nor depth, nor anything else in all creation, will be able to separate us from the love of God that is in Christ Jesus our Lord" (Rom. 8:38–39) and that "all things God works for the good of those who love him" (Rom. 8:28).

| | Moved | Redeemed |
|---|---|---|
| **JOSEPH** | Joseph moved from Canaan to Egypt.<br><br>He moved from being a spoiled, foolish young man to being a wise man.<br><br>He moved from anger and forgetfulness to forgiveness and restoration. | Joseph is redeemed from his sufferings in Egypt.<br><br>He is redeemed from being the victim of violence and injustice from his brothers.<br><br>He is redeemed from his own anger and memories.<br><br>He is redeemed by learning wisdom and trusting in God. |
| **JACOB** | Jacob moved from being the deceiver to being deceived.<br><br>He moved from the joy of his favorite son to the tragedy of Joseph's supposed death.<br><br>He moved from being a man defeated to being a man with a future. | Jacob is redeemed by receiving God's renewed promise.<br><br>Though Jacob had become a broken man, God's gracious acts through Joseph allow Jacob to have a renewed sense of hope for the future. This hope includes the promises that God made to Abraham. |
| **JOSEPH'S BROTHERS** | Joseph's brothers moved from their wicked deeds to willingness to accept their responsibility. | Joseph's brothers are redeemed from their early, evil ways. |
| **JUDAH** | Judah moved from being a man merely concerned with his own well-being to one willing to accept the consequences of his actions. He became the leader of the children of Israel. | Judah is redeemed from his previous egotism.<br><br>When Jacob blesses his children, Judah receives this blessing: "The scepter will not depart from Judah, nor the ruler's staff from between his feet" (Gen. 49:10).<br><br>From Judah, King David would be born, and later Jesus the promised Messiah, the one who fulfilled God's promises. |

# LIFE OF JOSEPH TIME LINE

**BIRTH OF JOSEPH**
Joseph is born in Mesopotamia to Jacob and Rachel, the eleventh son of Jacob. Gen. 30:22–24

Jacob moves his family to Canaan. Gen. 31:17–18

Resisting the sexual advances of Potiphar's wife, Joseph is thrown into prison after she falsely accuses him. Gen. 39:1–20

Joseph interprets the dreams of his fellow inmates—a cupbearer and a baker. Gen. 39:21–40:23

Joseph (age 17) tells his brothers about a dream he had in which they all bow down to him. In response, his jealous brothers sell him to slave traders and tell their father that he was killed by a wild animal. Gen. 37:5–35

Pharaoh renames Joseph as Zaphenath-Paneah and Joseph marries Asenath, the daughter of an Egyptian priest. Gen. 41:45

**1914 BC**

**1897 BC**

**1884 BC**

Rachel dies giving birth to Joseph's only younger brother Benjamin. Gen. 35:16–20

**JOSEPH IN EGYPT**
Joseph is sold to Potiphar, the captain of Pharaoh's guard. Gen. 37:36

Two years later, God enables Joseph to interpret Pharaoh's dream about seven years of plenty followed by seven years of famine. Gen. 41:1–38

Jacob favors Joseph, giving him an ornate robe that stirs up jealousy from his brothers. Gen. 37:2–4

**JOSEPH'S RISE TO POWER**
Pharaoh puts Joseph (age 30) in charge of his palace and all the land of Egypt to prepare for the famine. Gen. 41:39–52

In Egypt, Joseph's brothers bow down to him, seeking grain, but they do not recognize their brother. So Joseph tests them to see if they have changed.
Gen. 42:6–44:17

Joseph mourns his father's death and buries him in Canaan.
Gen. 49:29–50:14

Years later, just before his death, Joseph has the Israelites swear to one day carry his remains out of Egypt to be buried in Canaan. Gen. 50:22–25

**RECONCILIATION**
When Joseph's brothers demonstrate humility and self-sacrifice, Joseph can no longer keep up the deception. He reveals his identity and reconciles with his brothers.
Gen. 44:18–45:15

**DEATH OF JOSEPH**
Joseph dies at age 110 and is placed in a coffin in Egypt.
Gen. 50:26

1876 BC    1859 BC

When the seven years of plenty end and the years of famine begin, Jacob sends his sons to Egypt to purchase grain. Gen. 41:53–42:5

By selling grain during the famine, Joseph enriches and strengthens Pharaoh in all of Egypt.
Gen. 47:13–26

Joseph and his wife have two sons, Manasseh and Ephraim.
Gen. 41:50–52

**ISRAEL IN EGYPT**
Joseph's father Jacob (also named Israel) and brothers and their families migrate to Egypt. Gen. 45:16–47:12

About four centuries later, when Moses leads the Israelites out of Egypt, they bring with them Joseph's bones, which are laid to rest in Canaan.
Ex. 13:19; Josh. 24:32

Dates are approximate.

119

# CHAPTER 7

# Who's Who in Genesis

## Abel
GEN. 4:1–16

Abel was Adam and Eve's second son. He was a shepherd and he presented to God offerings from his flock—an act that pleased God and made Abel's brother Cain jealous. Abel was killed by Cain, making this the first murder in the book of Genesis.

## Abimelek
GEN. 20:1–18; 21:22–32; 26:1–31

*Abimelek* was the title for kings in Philistia. Abraham had an unexpected encounter with King Abimelek of Gerar in which Abraham lied about his wife Sarah's identity. Abimelek sent for Sarah, but God quickly revealed that Sarah was married. Abimelek released her and spoke with Abraham who prayed to God on the king's behalf. During a famine, Abraham's son Isaac lived in Philistia as well, though likely under a different King Abimelek. The same scene played out with Isaac and his wife. When Abimelek discovered that Rebekah was Isaac's wife, he released her and threatened death to anyone who would harm them.

## Abraham (Abram)
GEN. 11:26–13:18; 15:4–6; 17:9–19; 21:1–6; 22:1–19; 24:35; 25:1–8

God called Abraham to leave all that was familiar and journey to the land of Canaan. Although Abraham's wife Sarah was barren, God made a covenant with Abraham, promising to make him into a great nation and bless all nations of the earth through him. God changed his name from Abram to Abraham, meaning "father of many." Abraham believed God, and God considered him righteous because of his faith. When Abraham was 100 years old, Sarah gave birth to God's promised son, Isaac. Abraham traveled throughout Canaan and lived in Shechem, the hill country, Egypt during a famine, Bethel, the Negev Desert, and Hebron.

The Lord blessed him with abundant flocks, loyal servants, and wealth. After Sarah died, Abraham married Keturah and had six sons. Abraham gave them gifts but made Isaac his only heir before he died at age 175.

## Adam
GEN. 2:7–4:2, 25; 5:1–5

Adam was the first man. God created him from "the dust of the ground." Adam's name is related to the Hebrew word for "ground." God placed Adam in the garden of Eden to care for it. God created Eve, a suitable helpmate, from one of Adam's ribs. Adam and Eve enjoyed fellowship with God and each other until they rebelled against their Creator. The result was utter disaster, introducing sin and death into the world. God banished the couple from the garden and punished Adam with painful toil for the rest of his life. Adam was the father of Cain, Abel, Seth, and other children. He died at age 930.

## Asenath
GEN. 41:45, 50–52

Asenath was Joseph's wife and the daughter of an important Egyptian priest. She gave birth to Manasseh and Ephraim.

## Asher
GEN. 30:12–13

Asher was the eighth son of Jacob, and born to Leah's servant Zilpah. Leah chose his name, which means "happy," to reflect how she felt after he was born.

## Benjamin
GEN. 35:18, 24; 42:4–45:7

Benjamin was Jacob's twelfth and final son. His name means "son of the right hand." His mother Rachel died giving birth to him. Jacob reluctantly sent Benjamin to Egypt with his brothers to buy grain during a famine, where, unbeknownst to him, Joseph awaited them. Eventually, Benjamin, as well as the rest of the family, migrated and settled in Egypt where Joseph looked after them.

## Bethuel
GEN. 22:20–23; 24:47–51

Bethuel was Abraham's nephew, the son of Abraham's brother Nahor. Bethuel's children included Rebekah (Isaac's wife) and Laban (the father of Rachel and Leah).

## Bilhah
GEN. 29:29; 30:1–8; 35:21–22

Bilhah was the servant of Jacob's wife Rachel. After Jacob's other wife Leah bore Jacob four children, Rachel grew jealous because she was not conceiving. Rachel had Bilhah sleep with Jacob so she could claim Bilhah's children as her own. Bilhah gave birth to Dan and Naphtali.

## Cain
GEN. 4:1–16

Cain was Adam and Eve's first son. He was a farmer, and when he brought God an offering from his crops, God rejected it because his heart was faithless. Cain grew angry and jealous of his brother Abel, whose sacrifice was accepted by God. Cain spitefully killed his brother. God punished Cain by sending him far from home, forced to wander and face danger. Yet God was merciful and placed a mark on Cain that warned others not to kill him.

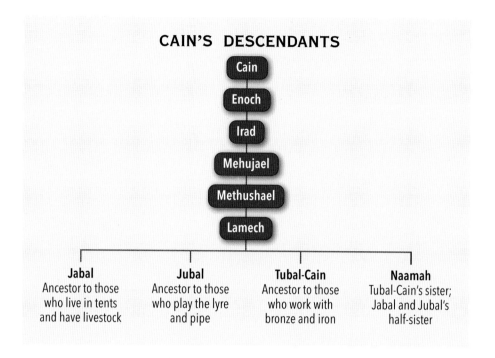

## CAIN'S DESCENDANTS

Cain → Enoch → Irad → Mehujael → Methushael → Lamech

**Jabal**
Ancestor to those who live in tents and have livestock

**Jubal**
Ancestor to those who play the lyre and pipe

**Tubal-Cain**
Ancestor to those who work with bronze and iron

**Naamah**
Tubal-Cain's sister; Jabal and Jubal's half-sister

## Dan

GEN. 30:1–6; 49:16–17

Dan was Jacob's fifth son and the first son born to Rachel's servant Bilhah. On his deathbed, Jacob prophesied that Dan would "provide justice for his people" (Gen. 49:16).

## Dinah

GEN. 34:1–31

Dinah was Jacob and Leah's young daughter who was defiled by Shechem, a Hivite. Two of Dinah's brothers deceitfully bargained with Shechem to give Dinah to him in marriage, but instead the brothers brutally murdered every male in Shechem's city. The Bible does not say what happened to Dinah after this terrible experience.

## Eliezar

GEN. 15:1–4; 24:1–67

As Abraham's oldest servant, Eliezar of Damascus was in charge of everything Abraham owned. Knowing he was trustworthy, Abraham sent Eliezar to find a wife for his son Isaac in the place where Abraham's relatives lived. When Eliezar arrived, he prayed for help, and God directed him to Rebekah. Eliezar gave Rebekah many gifts, and she agreed to go with him to Canaan and marry Isaac.

## Enoch, Son of Cain
GEN. 4:17–18

Enoch was Cain's first son, after whom Cain named the city he built.

## Enoch, Son of Seth
GEN. 5:18–24

Enoch was a descendant of Adam's son Seth, a forefather of Noah, and the father of Methuselah. He was a humble man who walked faithfully with God. When Enoch was 365 years old, God took him to heaven without dying.

## Ephraim
GEN. 41:50–52; 48:1–20

Ephraim and his brother Manasseh were the sons of Joseph and his Egyptian wife Asenath. When Joseph's father Jacob was nearing death, Joseph brought his sons to him for a blessing. Though Ephraim was younger, Jacob prophesied that Ephraim's descendants would be even greater than Manasseh's. Jacob blessed Ephraim, whose name means "double fruitfulness," with the birthright of the firstborn (a double portion of inheritance).

## Esau
GEN. 25:19–34; 27:1–45; 33:1–17; 36:1–9

Esau was the firstborn son of Isaac and Rebekah, and Jacob's twin. Famished after a long day of hunting, Esau traded his birthright for a bowl of stew Jacob had made. When Jacob tricked their father into giving him the firstborn blessing, Esau was furious and planned to kill Jacob, but Jacob fled. When Jacob returned twenty years later, the brothers were peacefully reunited. Esau's descendants were known as the Edomites, and they eventually became enemies of Jacob's descendants, the Israelites (Ezek. 35:1–15).

## Eve
GEN. 2:15–3:16, 20; 4:1–2, 25; 5:4

God fashioned Eve, the first woman, from Adam's rib, then presented her to Adam as his wife. Eve's name means "living" since she is the mother of all who live. Deceived by an evil serpent into disobeying God, she and Adam were punished by being banished from the garden of Eden. Eve later became the mother of Cain, Abel, Seth, and other children.

## Gad
GEN. 30:9–11

Gad was the seventh son of Jacob, and born to Leah's servant Zilpah. Upset that she had not conceived again after the birth of her fourth son, Leah gave Zilpah to Jacob to bear children for her.

## Hagar
GEN. 16:1–16; 21:8–21

Hagar was Sarah's Egyptian slave (maidservant). When Sarah could not conceive, she urged her husband Abraham to sleep with Hagar so he could have God's promised son. Hagar gave birth to a son named Ishmael, but God later revealed Abraham's promised son would be born to Sarah.

Hagar and Ishmael had a contentious relationship with Abraham's family and were eventually sent away, yet God provided for them in the wilderness.

## Isaac

GEN. 17:15–19; 21:1–7; 24:62–67; 25:19–26; 26:23–33; 27:1–40; 35:27–29

Born to Abraham and Sarah in their old age, Isaac was the son God had promised. Through Isaac's descendants, Abraham would become the

father of many nations. Isaac married Rebekah when he was forty. At age sixty, he became the father of twins Esau and Jacob. When Isaac was old and nearly blind, he was tricked into giving the firstborn blessing to Jacob instead of Esau. Isaac spent much of his life in Beersheba and Hebron, and God blessed him with wealth and favor.

## Ishmael

GEN. 16:1–16; 21:8–21

Ishmael was Abraham's first son, born to Hagar. When Ishmael was a teenager, he mocked Abraham and Sarah's son Isaac. Abraham and Sarah sent Hagar and Ishmael away, but God provided for them as they lived in the desert and promised to multiply Ishmael's descendants. Hagar arranged an Egyptian wife for Ishmael. Although Ishmael helped Isaac bury their father, his life was characterized by hostility toward his relatives.

## Issachar

GEN. 30:14–18

Issachar was the ninth son of Jacob, and born to Leah. He was conceived after Rachel traded with Leah a night with Jacob for Leah's son Reuben's mandrakes. Rachel was barren, and mandrakes were thought to aid conception.

# Jacob (Israel)

GEN. 25:19–34; 27:1–31:21; 32:22–32; 46:1–50:14

Jacob was Isaac's son and a grandson of Abraham, and the husband of sisters Leah and Rachel. God chose Jacob to fulfill the promises of land and children that he had made to Abraham and Isaac. Jacob's name means "he deceives," and Jacob lived up to it, often tricking members of his own family. After wrestling with God in a divine encounter, God renamed Jacob *Israel*, which means "he struggles with God." When Jacob was old, he moved with his family to Egypt to live near his son Joseph, who provided food for them during a famine. Jacob died at 147 years old and was buried in Abraham's family tomb in Hebron. The descendants of Jacob's twelve sons became the twelve tribes of Israel.

## SONS OF JACOB AND THEIR SONS

**1. Reuben**
Hanok
Pallu
Hezron
Karmi

**2. Simeon**
Jemuel   Jakin
Jamin    Zohar
Ohad     Shaul
   Hezron   Hemul

**3. Levi**
Gershon
Kohath
Merari

**4. Judah**
Er
Onan
Shelah
Zerah
Perez

**5. Dan**
Hashum

**6. Naphtali**
Jahziel
Guni
Jezer
Shillem

**7. Gad**
Zephon   Eri
Haggi    Arodi
Shuni    Areli
Ezbon

**8. Asher**
Imnah    Ishvi
Ishvah   Serah
         Beriah
   Heber   Malkiel

**9. Issachar**
Tola
Puah
Jashub
Shimron

**10. Zebulun**
Sered
Elon
Jahleel

**11. Joseph**
Manasseh
Ephraim

**12. Benjamin**
Bela     Ehi
Beker    Rosh
Ashbel   Muppim
Gera     Huppim
Naaman   Ard

## Joseph

GEN. 30:22–24; 37:1–36; 39:1–50:26

Joseph was Jacob's eleventh son, the first child Rachel bore. Favored by his father and despised by his brothers, Joseph's jealous siblings sold him as a slave. Joseph ended up in Egypt where he was falsely accused and imprisoned. But God watched over him and granted him favor. After interpreting Pharaoh's dreams, Joseph was made second in command of Egypt. Joseph married Asenath and had two sons, Manasseh and Ephraim. During a severe famine, Joseph sold grain to all who came to him, including his own brothers. They enjoyed a tearful reunion, and at Joseph's urging, Jacob's family migrated to Egypt. They had many years together before Joseph died at age 110.

## Judah

GEN. 29:31, 35; 37:18–28; 38

Judah was Jacob's fourth son, and born to Leah. Judah convinced his brothers not to kill Joseph but to sell him a slave instead. Later, Judah fathered twin sons with his widowed daughter-in-law Tamar. Judah is listed in the genealogy of Jesus in Matthew 1:1–3.

## Laban

GEN. 24:29; 29:14–30; 31:1–55

Laban was Jacob's uncle and the father of Rachel and Leah. After Jacob worked seven years for Rachel's hand in marriage, Laban tricked him into marrying Leah instead. Laban then required Jacob work for him seven more years for Rachel. Laban and Jacob's relationship was fraught with unfair dealings, but when Jacob left for Canaan, they agreed to part ways and treat each other with respect in any future dealings.

## Lamech
GEN. 4:18–24

Lamech was a descendant of Cain. He took two wives, Adah and Zillah. Like Cain, Lamech committed a murder. He even boasted about it, claiming that anyone who killed him in revenge would be punished seventy times more than Cain. Each of Lamech's sons contributed to the development of culture: Jabal was the first to be a tent dweller and raise livestock; Jubal was the first to play the flute and harp; and Tubal-cain made tools from bronze and iron.

## Leah
GEN. 29:16–30:21; 48:7; 49:29–31

Leah was Jacob's first wife. She shared Jacob with her beautiful younger sister Rachel, who was Jacob's favorite. Leah, described in the Bible as having "weak" eyes, felt unloved. To comfort her, God granted her children. But when she could not conceive, she gave her servant Zilpah to her husband to have children through her. Leah died after Rachel but before Jacob, who buried her in Abraham's family tomb in Hebron.

## Levi
GEN. 29:34; 49:5–7

Levi was Jacob's third son, and born to Leah. Jacob's blessing to Levi (and also Simeon) was a rebuke of Levi's fierce temper and violence. Levi's descendants became a tribe of priests for Israel (Num. 3:5–10).

## Lot
GEN. 11:31; 13:1–14; 14:1–16; 18:16–19:38

Lot was Abraham's nephew. When God called Abraham and Sarah to go to Canaan, Lot went with them. To avoid fights between their families and herdsmen, Abraham gave Lot his first choice of living locations. Lot chose the well-watered plains near Sodom. When war broke out in the area, Lot was captured, but Abraham rallied to rescue him. Lot and his family were also saved from God's destruction of Sodom, but Lot's wife looked back and became a "pillar of salt." When Lot and his daughters lived in the mountains with no prospects for continuing the family line, the daughters got their father drunk and slept with him, and both became pregnant. Their descendants, the Moabites and Ammonites, were enemies of the Israelites.

## Manasseh
GEN. 41:50–51; 48:1–20

Manasseh was the eldest son of Joseph with his Egyptian wife Asenath. Manasseh's name means "to forget," since, as Joseph explained, "God has made me forget all my trouble and all my father's household." Manasseh's younger brother was Ephraim, and the descendants of both brothers became tribes of Israel.

## Melchizedek
GEN. 14:18–20

Melchizedek's name means "king of righteousness." He was the king of Salem (possibly Jerusalem) and a priest of God. After Abraham rescued Lot and his possessions, Melchizedek brought Abraham bread and wine and gave him a special blessing. In return, Abraham gave Melchizedek a tenth of the spoils he took.

## Methuselah
GEN. 5:21–27

Methuselah was an ancestor of Noah. He died at the age of 969, which is the longest life span recorded in the Bible.

## Nahor
GEN. 11:26–29; 22:20–23; 24:1–28

Nahor was Abraham's brother and also a son of Terah. (His grandfather's name was also Nahor; Gen. 11:22–25.) It was important to Abraham that his son Isaac not marry a Canaanite, so he sent his servant to seek a bride from his brother Nahor's family in Paddan Aram. Genesis 24:28 says that Isaac's future wife Rebekah ran to tell "her mother's household" when the servant arrived, so it is possible that by this point in the Genesis narrative, Nahor had died.

## Naphtali
GEN. 30:7–8

Naphtali was the sixth son of Jacob, and born to Rachel's servant Bilhah. His name means "my struggle" and reflects Rachel's childbearing competition with Leah.

## Nephilim
GEN. 6:4

*Nephilim* is a Hebrew word that can mean "bully" or "giant," and may be related to a verb meaning "to fall." There has been much debate about what this word means in Genesis 6:4—"The Nephilim were on the earth in those days ... when the sons of God went to the daughters of humans and had children by them. They were the heroes of old, men of renown." One theory is that the Nephilim were the half-human offspring of angels and women. Another suggestion is that because of occult practices, demonic spirits would inhabit men and make them exceedingly powerful. In ancient literature, these superhuman people were referred to as "sons of god." Another interpretation is that "sons of God" in Genesis refers to the godly descendants of Seth who married ungodly women (possibly the descendants of Cain), and as a result, their offspring, the Nephilim, were those who "fell away."

## Nimrod

GEN. 10:8–12

Nimrod was a descendant of Noah's grandson Cush. He became a powerful king, warrior, and hunter. Nimrod's kingdom included Babylon and Assyria, where he built the city of Nineveh.

## Noah

GEN. 6:9–9:17, 29

During a time of extreme wickedness, God decided to send a devastating flood to destroy all living things—except righteous Noah and his family. Noah did as he was instructed by God: he built an ark, entered it with his family and many animals, and waited until the floodwaters came and then receded. The Lord made one of the first covenants in the Bible with Noah, promising to never again send a flood to destroy all living creatures. Noah had three sons and died at the age of 950.

## Pharaoh

GEN. 12:10–20; 41:37–44; 47:1–12; 50:1–14

*Pharaoh* was the title for the kings of Egypt, and Egypt was one of the most powerful empires of the ancient world. There are two pharaohs mentioned in Genesis, but both go unnamed. Abraham encounters Pharaoh when he travels to Egypt to escape a famine and lies about his wife's identity. Years later, Joseph, Abraham's great-grandson, becomes Pharaoh's chief official in all the land after interpreting Pharaoh's dreams.

## Potiphar

GEN. 37:36; 39:1–20

Potiphar was the captain of Pharaoh's guard. When Joseph's brothers sold him as a slave, Potiphar bought Joseph to serve in his house. Potiphar noticed Joseph's excellent work and put him in charge of his household.

God blessed Potiphar's affairs because of Joseph. This changed, however, when Potiphar's wife falsely accused Joseph of assaulting her. Potiphar had Joseph thrown into prison.

## Rachel
GEN. 29:1–30:24; 31:19–35; 35:16–20; 48:7

Rachel, the beautiful daughter of Laban, was shepherding her father's sheep when Jacob first met her and fell in love. Jacob eventually married Rachel but was deceived into marrying her older sister Leah first. Rachel was barren for a long time until God blessed her with her first son: Joseph. Rachel died giving birth to her second child Benjamin. Jacob grieved heavily and set up a monument over her tomb, located near Bethlehem.

## Rebekah
GEN. 24:1–67; 25:19–28; 27:1–46; 49:29–32

When Abraham sent his servant to find a wife for his son Isaac, God made it clear he had chosen Rebekah. She demonstrated kindness and a servant's heart by offering water to Abraham's servant and his camels. She willingly made the journey to Canaan and married Isaac. Rebekah struggled with infertility for twenty years, but God answered Isaac's prayers and gave Rebekah twin sons: Esau and Jacob. She favored Jacob and deceived Isaac in his old age into giving Jacob the blessing of the firstborn. The Bible does not record the details of Rebekah's death, but it mentions that she was buried with Isaac in Abraham's family tomb.

## Reuben
GEN. 29:31–32; 37:12–36; 49:3–4

Reuben was Jacob's first son, and born to Leah. Reuben tried to rescue Joseph when the rest of his brothers wanted to kill him. Reuben also slept with Bilhah, Jacob's concubine, so Jacob took away Reuben's birthright.

## Sarah (Sarai)

GEN. 11:29–12:20; 17:15–21; 18:10–15; 20:1–18; 21:1–7; 23:1–20

Sarah, Abraham's wife, was barren for many years. When the Lord revealed that she would bear a son in her old age, Sarah laughed at this news. But a year later, she gave birth to Isaac, whose name means "laughter." Sarah was also known for her beauty. Two foreign kings wanted to take her as a wife but released her when they discovered she was married to Abraham. Sarah died at age 127 and was buried in Hebron.

## Seth

GEN. 4:25–5:3

Seth was Adam and Eve's third son. His name means "granted." Eve chose this name since God granted her another child after her son Cain killed her son Abel. Seth had a son named Enosh, whose family line includes Noah, Abraham, Jacob, and Jesus Christ (Luke 3:23–38).

## Shem, Ham, and Japheth

GEN. 5:32; 6:17–18; 9:20–27

Shem, Ham, and Japheth were Noah's sons who entered the ark with their wives. After the flood, their father got drunk and lay naked in his tent.

Ham discovered that Noah was naked and told his brothers. Shem and Japheth covered their father's nakedness with a garment. This incident caused Noah to curse and bless his sons, saying that Ham's son Canaan would serve his brothers.

# TABLE OF NATIONS
## GENESIS 10

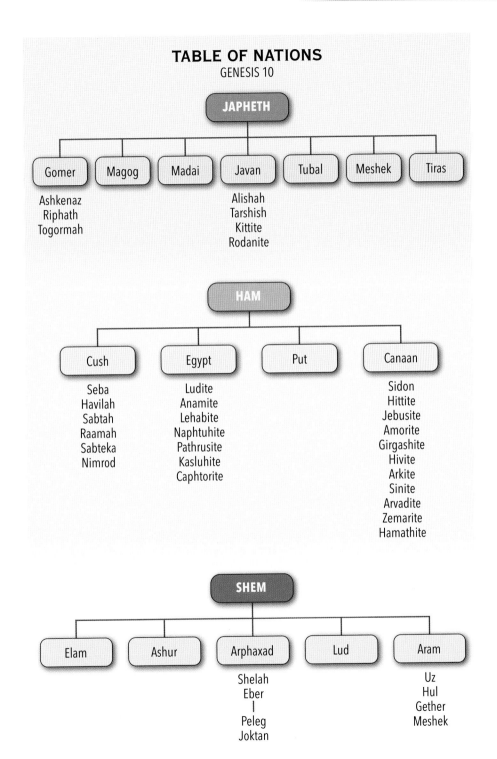

**JAPHETH**

| Gomer | Magog | Madai | Javan | Tubal | Meshek | Tiras |

Ashkenaz
Riphath
Togormah

Alishah
Tarshish
Kittite
Rodanite

**HAM**

| Cush | Egypt | Put | Canaan |

Seba
Havilah
Sabtah
Raamah
Sabteka
Nimrod

Ludite
Anamite
Lehabite
Naphtuhite
Pathrusite
Kasluhite
Caphtorite

Sidon
Hittite
Jebusite
Amorite
Girgashite
Hivite
Arkite
Sinite
Arvadite
Zemarite
Hamathite

**SHEM**

| Elam | Ashur | Arphaxad | Lud | Aram |

Shelah
Eber
|
Peleg
Joktan

Uz
Hul
Gether
Meshek

## Simeon
GEN. 29:33; 34:1–26; 42:1–43:23; 49:5–7

Simeon was Jacob's second son, and born to Leah. Simeon and his brother Levi killed the residents of Shechem to avenge their sister Dinah. Later, when Simeon went with his brothers to buy grain in Egypt, Joseph held him as a prisoner until his brothers returned with Benjamin. Jacob's deathbed blessing to Simeon and and Levi was a rebuke of their violence.

## Tamar
GEN. 38:6–30

Tamar was the daughter-in-law of Judah. When Tamar's husband (Judah's eldest son) died, she married Judah's middle son. When he also died, Judah promised Tamar that she would marry his third son when he came of age.

When Tamar realized that Judah was not going to follow through with his promise, she came up with her own plan to preserve her husband's name and family line. She disguised herself as a prostitute and waited by the road. When Judah came along, she slept with him and became pregnant. Tamar gave birth to twin sons: Perez and Zerah. Perez is an ancestor of Jesus, and Tamar is one of only five women mentioned in Jesus's genealogy (Matt. 1:3).

## Terah
GEN. 11:27–32

Terah was the father of Abraham, Nahor, and Haran. (Terah may also have been the father or a close relative of Sarah, though a precise blood relation remains uncertain; Gen. 20:12). After his son Haran died in the land of Ur, Terah and his family set out on a long trip toward the land of Canaan. Before completing the journey, however, they decided to settle in Harran in upper Mesopotamia. Terah died there at the age of 205.

## Zebulun

GEN. 30:19–20

Zebulun was the tenth son of Jacob and the youngest son of Leah. His name probably means "honor." Because Leah had already given Jacob several sons, she hoped that Jacob would treat her with honor after Zebulun's birth.

## Zilpah

GEN. 29:21–24; 30:9–13

Zilpah was Leah's servant. After Leah bore Jacob four sons, she became barren and gave Zilpah to Jacob to have children through her. Zilpah gave birth to Gad and Asher, but Leah counted them as her own sons.

# CHAPTER 8

# Seeing Christ in Genesis

Jesus Christ is the key to what God had been pointing to in all the history of God's people. When he was confronted by religious leaders who read the Hebrew Scriptures but did not believe in him, Jesus said to them:

> These are the very Scriptures that testify about me, yet you refuse to come to me to have life…. If you believed Moses, you would believe me, for he wrote about me.
>
> JOHN 5:39–40, 46

There are many different ways to see how the Old Testament anticipates, reveals, promises, or foreshadows Christ. One of those ways is to examine parallels between people, events, and things in the Old Testament and the life of Jesus in the New Testament. Take for example, the parallels of Adam and Christ that the apostle Paul wrote about in his letters. In Romans 5, Paul states that sin came into the world through Adam, and sin led to death for all humankind: "Therefore, just as sin entered the world through one man, and death through sin, and in this way death came to all people, because all sinned" (Rom. 5:12). Paul also says that Adam was a figure of someone who would appear later: "Adam … is a pattern of the one to come" (Rom. 5:14). Paul goes on to explain that if the sin of one person (Adam) would cause many to die, how much more would the gift of God's grace by one person (Jesus Christ) cause many to be righteous and have eternal life (Rom. 5:17). In his letter to the Corinthians, Paul reiterates this message:

> For since death came through a man, the resurrection of the dead comes also through a man. For as in Adam all die, so in Christ all will be made alive.
>
> 1 CORINTHIANS 15:21–22

The Bible is full of these parallels or *types*. The study of types is called typology. Adam is a good example of a type because this example shows clearly that typology focuses on specific life events or character traits rather than on the person as a whole. There are big differences between Adam and Christ; in fact, they are opposites of one another. So it is not that Adam was Christ-like; rather, some features of Adam's story parallel

Christ's life and ministry—some of which are positive and others negative. In typology, Adam is the type and Christ is the antitype (opposite).

Typology was a very common way to interpret the Old Testament in the early history of the church. When carefully done, typology opens windows into the history of God's activity in the world that otherwise can be easily missed. Augustine of Hippo, a fourth-century theologian, explained, "The New Testament is in the Old concealed; the Old Testament is in the New revealed."

Typology can also include parallels between events and things, not just people. For example, the exodus event, in which God rescues the Israelites from slavery in Egypt, anticipates how Christ frees us from the slavery of sin (John 8:34–36; Gal. 5:1). John 1:14 connects the Old Testament tabernacle, where God dwelt with his people in the wilderness, with Jesus dwelling (literally, "tabernacling") among us when he came to earth.

By looking for parallels or similarities between biblical people, events, and things, we can see God setting up history for the coming of Christ and doing it not simply by speaking a prophetic word, but by arranging the affairs of human beings. When we understand this great truth, we can have hope that our own lives also point to Christ and rejoice in the Lord of history who makes such wonderful stories of us!

*This chapter compares five key figures from the book of Genesis with the life and ministry of Jesus Christ: Adam, Noah, Abraham, Melchizedek, and Joseph.*

# ADAM

Adam was the first human God created. He was responsible to care for the garden of Eden. His disobedience of God's commandment introduced sin and death, so humanity and all of creation became corrupted by sin.

| ADAM | CHRIST |
|------|--------|
| Adam was the first person in this creation (Gen. 2:7). | In his resurrection, Jesus is the first person in this new creation (1 Cor. 15:23). |
| Adam was called the son of God (Luke 3:38). | Christ is the Son of God (John 1:14). |
| Adam was God's administrator or ruler (Gen. 1:28). | Christ is God's anointed to be king (Matt. 1:16). |
| Adam was the head of the race (Gen. 3:20). | Christ Jesus is the head of the new creation (Rom. 5:12–24). |
| His actions brought consequences to his children causing them to inherit sin and death (Gen. 3:16–19). | His actions brought consequences to God's children causing them to inherit righteousness and life (Rom. 5:12–19; 1 Cor. 15:20–22, 45–49). |
| Adam joined Eve and rebelled against God (Gen. 3:6). | Christ redeemed his bride (the church) by obeying God (Rev. 19:7–9). |
| Adam's shame required the death of an animal to cover it (Gen. 3:21). | Christ was shamed, stripped, and slain to cover our shame (Matt. 27:27–35). |
| Instead of closeness with God, we experience isolation and loneliness. Instead of love and care for each other, we experience violence and hatred. | Through Christ's redemptive action, we can experience true life, a close relationship with God and his love, and care for others. |

# NOAH

When God had decided to destroy the world with a flood as a punishment for humanity's sin, God chose to save Noah and his family.

| NOAH | CHRIST |
|---|---|
| Noah was a kind of "second Adam" since all living human beings come from him (Gen. 8:15–9:17). | Christ is called "the second man" (Adam) since eternal life can only be found in him (1 Cor. 15:47). |
| Noah's ark provided refuge for all kinds of animals (Gen. 6:19–7:5). | Christ's body (the church) provides salvation for all, both Jew and gentile (Rom. 11:11; Gal. 3:28–29). |
| Human evil had reached an unacceptable high. So God decided to undo his creation with a flood (Gen. 6:6–7). | When the time is right for God, he will undo his creation by fire to re-create it (2 Peter 3:12–13; Rev. 21:1). |
| Noah's ark was delivered from the flood waters (Gen. 7:7). | Christ's body (the church) was delivered from death through the water of baptism (1 Peter 3:21). |
| Noah offered a sacrifice of blood (Gen. 8:20–9:6). | Christ offered himself as a sacrifice (1 Peter 1:18–19). |
| Noah's ark came to rest on Mount Ararat on the Jewish month of Nisan 17 (Gen. 8:4). | Christ's resurrection took place on Nisan 17 (which corresponds to the month of March or April). |
| Although Noah was not perfect, he is described as a "righteous man, blameless among the people of his time, and he walked with God" (Gen. 6:9). | Jesus was the perfect, blameless man (Heb. 4:15). |

# ABRAHAM

God promised Abraham that he would be the father of a great nation and that his wife Sarah would give him a son. Through this son, God would bless all the nations. When they were elderly, Abraham and Sarah had Isaac, the son of the promise.

| ABRAHAM | CHRIST |
|---|---|
| Abraham is called the "Father of the Faith" (Gen.15; Rom. 4:16–18). | Christ is the author and perfecter of faith (Heb. 12:2). |
| Abraham was willing to sacrifice his only son, and Isaac was ready to do what his father said (Gen. 22:2, 9). | God the Father was willing to sacrifice his only Son, and Jesus was ready to do what his Father said (John 3:16; 10:17–18). |
| Abraham's faith allowed him to trust that God would keep his word, even if that meant raising Isaac from the dead (Heb. 11:17–19). | As Abraham's faith allowed him to look forward to Jesus's own resurrection with hope, we now look backward to that same resurrection that gives us hope (1 Cor. 15:54–58). |
| Abraham's sacrifice took place on Mount Moriah (Jerusalem; Gen. 22:2; 2 Chron. 3:1) and a ram was substituted for Isaac (Gen. 22:8, 13–14). | Christ was sacrificed on the outskirts of Jerusalem (John 19:17–18) and he is the Lamb of God (John 1:29–31). |
| Abraham's son (Isaac) was the child of the promise. The book of Hebrews connects Isaac to the idea of resurrection (Heb. 11:17–19). | God's Son Jesus is the child of promise who is resurrected (Isa. 9:6; 1 Cor. 15:1–11). |
| In Isaac's birth, all nations were to be blessed (Gen. 12:3). | In Jesus Christ all nations are blessed (Acts 28:28; Matt. 28:18–20). |

# MELCHIZEDEK

After Abraham came back from fighting enemy armies to free Lot, Melchizedek, king of Salem, met him on the road with a gift of bread and wine. Abraham recognized him as a fellow believer and a priest of the true God by giving to him one tenth of his earnings, which was the king's share (see 1 Sam. 8:15–17).

| MELCHIZEDEK | CHRIST |
|---|---|
| Melchizedek's name means "king of righteousness." | Christ is the Righteous One (Acts 3:14; Jer. 23:5-6). |
| Melchizedek was king of Salem (Jerusalem). The word "salem" means peace (Gen. 14:18; Heb. 7:2). He was king before David. | Christ is the Prince of Peace and the rightful king of Jerusalem for all time (Isa. 9:6-7). |
| Melchizedek was a priest of God Most High (Gen.14:18) before Aaron and the Levitical priesthood. (Aaron and his sons were ordained as the priestly family for Israel in Leviticus 8.) | Christ's high priesthood precedes and is superior to any other priesthood– that is, the priesthood of Aaron in Leviticus 8 and of Melchizedek in Genesis 14 (Heb. 7:4–10). |
| Old Testament priests offered blessings for God's people (Num. 6:22–27). | As the high priest, Christ blesses God's people with every spiritual blessing (Heb. 7:4–10; Eph. 1:3). |
| Melchizedek blessed Abraham on God's behalf (Gen. 14:19–20). | Christ blesses us, Abraham's spiritual children (Gal. 3:29). |

# JOSEPH

After Joseph's jealous brothers threw him into a pit, he was taken to Egypt and sold as a slave. In Egypt, God blessed Joseph, who became second only to the king of Egypt. God used Joseph to bless the nations by wisely storing up grain so that they were ready for a coming famine.

| JOSEPH | CHRIST |
|---|---|
| Joseph was rejected by his own brothers (Gen. 37:19–20). | Christ was rejected by his own (John 1:11). |
| Joseph was stripped of his robe, thrown into a pit, and sold into slavery (Gen. 37:22–28). | Christ was stripped of his robe and condemned to death (Matt. 27:27–31). |
| Joseph was sent to a dungeon (Gen. 39:20). | Christ descended to hell (1 Peter 3:18–20). |
| Joseph was an exemplary servant (Gen. 39:1–6). | Christ came as a humble servant (Phi. 2:7). |
| Though tempted, Joseph did not give in to sin (Gen. 39:7–12). | Though tempted, Christ did not sin (Heb. 4:15). |
| Joseph was unjustly accused and condemned (Gen. 39:13–20). | Christ was unjustly accused and condemned (Matt. 26:57–68; 27:11–25). |
| In prison, Joseph interpreted a dream of life to one of his fellow prisoners and death to another (Gen. 40:6–23). | While on the cross, his words promised life to one of the thieves condemned with him (Luke 23:39–43). |
| Joseph was raised out of the dungeon to sit at Pharaoh's right hand (Gen. 41:14–45). | Jesus was raised from the prison of death to sit at the right hand of God the Father (Acts 2:33; 5:31). |

| JOSEPH | CHRIST |
|--------|--------|
| Joseph had a meal with his brothers before he revealed his identity to them (Gen. 43:16). | Jesus had a last supper with his disciples (Matt. 26:17–30). After his death and resurrection, he revealed himself to them alive (Luke 24:1–49; 1 Cor. 15:1–11). |
| Joseph's actions saved the lives of his brothers, the people of Egypt, and the lives of many others (Gen. 45:3–15; 50:20). | Christ's actions brought about salvation for all who believe (John 3:16–18). |
| In Joseph, God partially fulfilled his promise to Abraham to bless all the nations of the world (Gen. 12:1–3), since Joseph's actions helped the nations of the world survive the terrible famine (Gen. 41:57). | In Christ, God completely fulfilled his promise to Abraham (Gen. 12:1–3), since Christ died for the sins of the world and Jesus commanded his followers to "go and make disciples of all nations" (Matt. 28:19). |

# PHOTOS AND ILLUSTRATIONS

p. 11 Mosaic of Abraham offering up Isaac in All Saints Church designed by Butterfield and painted by Alexander Gibbs (1873, London), Renata Sedmakova/Shutterstock; p. 43 Lifting up the Torah scroll at the Western Wall for Simchat Torah, John Theodor/Shutterstock; p. 70 Noah's Ark Replica at Ark Encounter in Williamstown, KY, May 29, 2017, ChicagoPhotographer/Shutterstock; p. 73 *L'arche de Noé* (mosaics of the Palatine Chapel, Palermo, Sicily), photo by Jean-Pierre DalbéraFollow/ flickr. p. 78 Tablet 11 of the Gilgamesh Epic, photo by Photograph by Mike Peel (www.mikepeel.net). Llyn Llydaw from Crib Goch (http://commons. wikimedia.org/wiki/File:Llyn_Llydaw_from_Crib_Goch_2.jpg) by Mike Peel (http://www.mikepeel.net/), licensed under CC BY-SA 4.0 (https:// creativecommons.org/licenses/by-sa/4.0/).

From *The Family Time Bible in Pictures* by Tyndale House Publishers, Inc.: p. 123 Adam and Eve copyright © 1989 by Joan Pelaez; p. 124 Cain and Abel copyright © 1989 by Blas Gallego; p. 127 copyright © 1989 by Joan Pelaez; p. 130 Joseph © 1989 by Joan Pelaez; p. 134 Noah copyright © 1989 by Blas Gallego.

Relief portions of maps by Michael Schmeling/www.aridocean.com.

# THE GOSPEL OF
# JOHN

## Finding Identity and Purpose

### 12-Session Video-Based Bible Study
Matt Williams, General Editor

**DVD** (ISBN: 9781628627879)

**Participant's Guide** (ISBN: 9781628627862)

**The Complete Kit** (ISBN: 9781628628296)

- ◆ DVD
- ◆ Participant's Guide
- ◆ *Rose Guide to the Gospels* (handbook)
- ◆ Leader's Guide (PDF on CD)
- ◆ *Life of Jesus Time Line* PowerPoint® (100+ slides on CD)

---

## More video Bible Studies by Matt Williams

*Deeper Connections* series (six sessions each):

> *The Prayers of Jesus* (ISBN: 9781628627688)
> *The Parables of Jesus* (ISBN: 9781628627640)
> *The Life of Jesus* (ISBN: 9781628624441)
> *The Forgiveness of Jesus* (ISBN: 9781628624403)
> *The Last Days of Jesus* (ISBN: 9781628624328)
> *The Miracles of Jesus* (ISBN: 9781628624304)

Visit www.hendricksonrose.com to see all Rose Publishing video series titles!

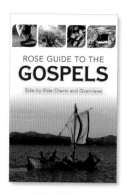

## ROSE GUIDE TO THE GOSPELS

Includes: key information about the uniqueness of each gospel; a harmony of the gospels; who's who in the gospels; background to the world of Jesus; evidence for the resurrection; and more.

ISBN 9781628628111

---

## ROSE GUIDE TO THE BOOK OF ACTS

Includes: overview of the book of Acts; understanding the message and background of Acts; life of the apostle Paul; who's who in Acts; time line and maps; the Holy Spirit in the lives of Christians; and more.

ISBN 9781649380203

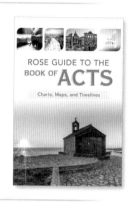

---

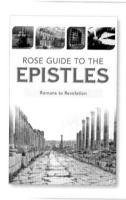

## ROSE GUIDE TO THE EPISTLES

Includes: overview of the epistles; key facts on each epistle at a glance; who's who in the epistles; the seven churches of Revelation; comparison of Christian views on the book of Revelation; and more.

ISBN 9781649380227

---

## ROSE GUIDE TO GENESIS

Includes: charts, maps, and time lines for the book of Genesis; stories of Noah's ark, Abraham, and Joseph; understanding the ancient world; who's who in Genesis; and more.

ISBN 9781496477996

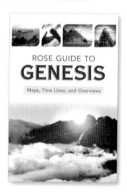

**www.hendricksonrose.com**